PSYCHOLOGY OF THE YOUTHFUL OFFENDER

Second Edition

PSYCHOLOGY OF THE YOUTHFUL OFFENDER

By

ROBERT N. WALKER, PH.D

Professor of Criminal Justice

Sam Houston State University

Huntsville, Texas

CHARLES C THOMAS • PUBLISHER
Springfield • Illinois • U.S.A.

Published and Distributed Throughout the World by

CHARLES C THOMAS · PUBLISHER

Bannerstone House

301-327 East Lawrence Avenue, Springfield, Illinois, U.S.A.

*With THOMAS BOOKS careful attention is given to all details of
manufacturing and design. It is the Publisher's desire to present books that are
satisfactory as to their physical qualities and artistic possibilities and
appropriate for their particular use. THOMAS BOOKS will be true to those
laws of quality that assure a good name and good will.*

HM
291
.W24
1973

Library of Congress Cataloging in Publication Data

Walker, Robert N
    Psychology of the youthful offender.

    1. Deviant behavior. 2. Adolescent psychology.
3. Juvenile delinquency. I. Title.   [DNLM:
1. Adolescent psychology. 2. Juvenile delinquency.
WS 462 W183p 1973]
HM291.W24   1973   301.6'2   73–6583
ISBN 0–398–02859–1

Printed in the United States of America
BB-14

Is man's civilization only a wrappage, through which the savage nature of him can still burst, infernal as ever?
... THOMAS CARLYLE

PREFACE

This textbook is the end product of over thirty years of university teaching, the past ten devoted exclusively to the interaction of the criminal justice system and deviant behavior in the United States.

The book is concerned with the essential social-psychological insights required for initial safety-minimum role enactment in police, corrections, fire, nursing, and social welfare transactions between professionals (and paraprofessionals) and the public.

The concise subject matter is offered as a semester length basic text for college, pre-college, and training academies. It can stand alone as a basic text in social psychology; courses in general or introductory psychology and social psychology would be excellent as foundation.

Deviant youthful behavior now comprises more than half of all cases compelling official cognizance by the criminal justice and social welfare agencies of our society. An understanding of the nature, motivations, and criminogenic factors operating in today's society is imperatively needed. This book is addressed to this need.

The author's debt to thousands of his students is gratefully acknowledged; colleagues in the Institute of Contemporary Corrections and the Behavioral Sciences of the Sam Houston State University, and previously, of the American University, also deserve credit; the book's deficiencies are solely those of the author. Mrs. Julie M. Sparkman, formerly with the Texas Department of Corrections, was indispensable in the preparation of the first edition. The second edition incorporates numerous suggestions from my students and colleagues, as a result of a second year of classroom use.

Necessarily, decisions were required relative to inclusion and omission of many facets of this subject matter; the central objective of the book, to present only essential aspects, precluded inclusion of much material.

ROBERT N. WALKER

FOREWORD

Every profession seems to have its own philosopher who can communicate with intelligence and simplicity on any condition of man. The trauma of man, during war and crime, has been the training camp for Robert N. Walker. Those already familiar with Dr. Walker's works will find an old friend in this selection of topics, which afford the reader an opportunity to glean from his lifetime of experiences and encounters. Strangers to the author will find this volume a comprehensive and easily readable introduction to the good and evil forces engaged in dramatic combat within the psyche of the juvenile offender.

A general practitioner of the study of human behavior since 1933, Walker has found the time and the talent to write on almost every aspect of the adolescent years through the eyes of his profession. *Psychology of the Youthful Offender* is a collection of pragmatic subject matter through four decades of continuing research. The uniting thread in all the chapters is his strong belief, reinforced by his extensive and varied experience, that there is an order and a logic to everything. The volume is, in fact, tangible verification of the old school maxim that the study and practice of juvenile psychology is a way of thought and reasoning with which to approach any and every topic relating to human behavior. On each subject, Walker stands away from the crowd, identifies the situation and arrives at a conclusion with a combination of logic, sensibility and the warmth and acumen of an artist.

For the layman, this volume presents an enjoyable and refreshing approach to a wide understanding of the behavior of the juvenile offender and for the criminal justice professional, probably that and much more. The juvenile whose behavior problems we fail to correct today becomes the criminal of tomorrow. If we, who represent ourselves to be the professionals in the field of criminal justice, can but understand and interpret the distress signals of despair from today's youth . . . and can stop even one delinquent career per year from developing, we will save our salary many times over.

We can afford no longer to be passive when we should be most active, in working to change the attitude of society, so that the emotionally disturbed youth may receive from us a *preventive medicine.* Society which is expending huge sums of money to protect itself from crime and its effects would also seem to need protection against its own actions, or inaction. Everyone in this field, and I do mean everyone—agencies, salaried and volunteer workers, government departments, custodians, supervisors, treatment staff—must accept the fact that the rehabilitation process does not finish when a man is released from prison . . . nor should we limit the perimeters of our profession to touch a human life, in the name of *rehabilitation,* only on a post-facto basis.

In attempting to educate the public to a better understanding, we must also educate and discipline ourselves, so that we do give the public the impression that we are in constant disagreement. As with other causes, however, it is the individual worker who must ultimately effect that change . . . a change that will be forthcoming if the worker realizes and heeds the dictates of this book.

GEORGE G. KILLINGER, Ph.D.
Director
Institute of Contemporary Corrections
And the Behavioral Sciences
Sam Houston State University

CONTENTS

PSYCHOLOGY OF THE YOUTHFUL OFFENDER

CHAPTER I

INTRODUCTION

THE YOUTHFUL OFFENDER as a recognized element of society is a social phenomenon which has developed in America during the past two decades. The rate of crimes perpetrated by youths has been steadily increasing at a rate exceeding population increases.

Seventy-five percent of all index crime arrests each year since 1960 were youths between the ages of 15 and 25, according to statistics published by the Federal Bureau of Investigation in its Uniform Crime Reports. The increase between 1960 and 1970 was 167 percent. (Index crimes are homicide, aggravated assault, forcible rape, robbery, burglary, larceny over $50, and auto theft.) Fifty percent of *all* crimes are now committed by persons under the age of 18. Arrests of juveniles under 18 for all types of offenses combined more than doubled between 1960 and 1970.

Juvenile Court Statistics, 1971, dated 7 December, 1972, from the U.S. Department of Health, Education, and Welfare, contains the latest available juvenile court statistics relative to children's cases disposed of by juvenile courts. Although admittedly it did not measure the full extent of delinquency, dependency, or neglect, over one million juvenile delinquency cases, excluding traffic offenses, were estimated as being handled by all juvenile courts in the United States in 1971. These children represent 2.9 percent of all children aged 10 through 17 in this country.

In 1971, there was again an increase in the number of juvenile court delinquency cases over the previous year. The increase for 1971 was 7 percent as compared to an increase in the child population aged 10 through 17 of only 1 percent.

3

Thus, the upward trend in the number of delinquency cases continues. And again, as in most previous years in the past decade, the increase exceeded the increase in the child population. Between 1960 and 1971, the number of juvenile delinquency cases more than doubled (121 percent increase) as compared to the 30 percent increase in the number of children aged 10 through 17. Each year since 1965, the percentage increase in delinquency cases was higher than the year before except for 1970, when the increase for that year was 6 percent as compared with the 10 percent increase for 1969.

All types of courts (urban, semi-urban, and rural) experienced increases in 1971—5, 12, and 11 percent respectively.

In 1971, police arrests of juveniles increased by 5 percent and as mentioned above, juvenile court cases increased by 7 percent. Perhaps half of the less serious juvenile offenses are diverted—handled non-judicially—by the arresting officer's curbside adjudication (admonition/warning), or the case is adjusted or referred to other community resources, adding an unknown proportion of additional adversary encounters between the police and youths of tender ages. Cases of dependency and neglect, numbering 130,900 in 1971, show further extensive involvement of children and youths with some aspect of the criminal justice system.

In the 1971 edition of Uniform Crime Reports, the Federal Bureau of Investigation reported that arrests of juveniles under 18 years of age, for all types of offenses combined, more than doubled (+125 percent) between 1960 and 1971. For a group of serious offenses selected as being most reliably reported (criminal homicide, forcible rape, burglary, robbery, aggravated assault, larceny, and auto theft), the combined increase between 1960 and 1971 was 107 percent. When offenses against the person (homicide, forcible rape, aggravated assault, and robbery), generally accepted as being the most serious crimes, are selected from the reliably reported group, the increase between 1960 and 1971 was 193 percent.

As determined from police arrest data, all types of offenses—serious as well as relatively minor—have been increasing with the most serious ones showing substantially greater proportionate increases. Serious offenses against persons, however, still only represent about 3 percent of all arrests of juveniles.

Delinquency remains primarily a boy's problem, but the disparity between the number of boys' and girls' delinquency court cases is narrowing. For many years, boys were referred to court for delinquency about four times as often as girls. Because of the recent faster increase in girls' cases as compared to boys', as outlined below, the ratio was reduced to three to one by 1971.

Nationally, girls' cases increased almost twice as much as did the boys' cases from 1970 to 1971. The girls' cases increased 11 percent as compared to a 6 percent increase for boys' cases.

Girls' delinquency cases disposed of by juvenile courts have been rising faster than those of boys' every year since 1965. Between 1965 and 1971, girls' delinquency cases increased by 97 percent whereas boys' cases increased by 52 percent.

Police arrest data also confirm that girls are participating in delinquency at a faster pace than boys. Between 1960 and 1971, arrests of girls under 18 years of age increased by 341 percent for "violent" crimes and by 278 percent for "property" crimes; for boys the percentage increases were 182 percent and 81 percent, respectively.

The rise in girls' delinquency has generally been attributed to their changing attitude towards society and society's changing attitude towards them. Instead of the passive role assumed by girls in the past and society's protective role towards them, girls are becoming more aggressive and more independent in their day-to-day activities. Unfortunately, some of this behavior has resulted in large increases in the incidences of running away from home and in participation in the use of drugs, often necessitating other crime-related activities, such as shoplifting, robbery, etc.

More than half (58 percent) of the delinquency cases disposed of by juvenile courts in 1971 were handled non-judicially (i.e. without the filing of a petition).

The proportion of delinquency cases handled nonjudicially is very large. Even though it may be appropriate to handle as many cases as possible in this manner, it raises the question as to why so many that do not require judicial determination should even come to the court's attention.

The rate of delinquency cases (the number of cases per 1,000 child population aged 10 through 17) was 34.1 in 1971 as compared to 32.3 in 1970. Between 1960 and 1971, the rate increased from 20.1 to 34.1. In 1971, the rate of delinquency cases was more than twice as high in predominantly urban areas as in rural areas.

JUVENILE DELINQUENCY CASES are those referred for acts defined in the statutes of the State as the violation of a State law or municipal ordinance by children or youth of juvenile court age, or for conduct so seriously antisocial as to interfere with the rights of others or to menace the welfare of the delinquent himself, or of the community. This broad definition of delinquency includes conduct which violates the law only when committed by children, e.g. truancy, ungovernable behavior, and running away.

METHOD OF HANDLING CASES is classified into judicial and nonjudicial, sometimes referred to as official and unofficial. "Judicial cases" are those where the court has acted on the basis of a petition or motion; "nonjudicial cases," consequently, are those cases which have been adjusted by the judge, referee, probation officer, or officer of the court without the invocation of the court's jurisdiction through petition or motion.

Why has this tremendous increase in juvenile crime come about? Who is this human being to whom we attach the label of juvenile offender?

Only by learning as much as we can about *who* is a juvenile offender can we answer the question of *why* is a juvenile offender. And only by answering the question of why he is a juvenile offender can we hope to reverse the trend toward youthful crime and perhaps channel this almost inexhaustible reservoir of power and intelligence toward constructive rather than destructive behavior.

Each individual is the unique product of his peculiar physical inheritance and the environmental shaping of that genetic endowment by social conditioning. No two individuals (other than identical twins) have the same physical endowment. Too, the environment, beginning even before conception, is unique for each individual. We are *not* born equal, nor do we have an equal chance to mature into productive, happy adults. We are all *programmed* by our ancestry, home, and school (or non-school) shapings, and many persons are in fact *locked-in* by shaping forces which they cannot control. This unfavorable environment operates most harmfully with the deprived and segregated residents of the so-called inner city areas—the ghetto—who are known as the *unpeople:* unhealthy, uneducated, unmotivated, unskilled, and unemployed.

Youths growing up in these disadvantaged settings have many built-in hurdles to overcome: poor health, overcrowded and unhygienic housing, broken families, second-rate schools with high drop-out rates, inadequate recreation, poor or non-available health services, and life-space associations which are negative or, at best, less than favorable in respect to exposure to criminal temptations. That the combination of these undesirable shaping forces results in antisocial behavior is not surprising.

Each of us is an omnibus in which our ancestors ride. If we could choose our ancestors, we might choose a little differently so that we might inherit more beauty, more intelligence, or a keener sense of humor; however, this is not for us to choose. We are blueprinted in advance by the nature and nurture of circumstances of our parents and our parents' parents. Thus, to a more or less degree, our lives are in a sense programmed. For some, the hurdles of life will prove too great to surmount; others rise above their limitations of ethnic and family milieu. We do, when we become of responsible age, enter the picture with choices that we, ourselves, make. But even then, the influences of the impressive teacher, a school counselor, a scout leader, a delinquent associate, or a neighbor can make a world of difference. The accidents of friendships or untoward contacts in our lives are highly significant, for favorable or unfavorable results. A story is often told in criminology courses about a long-legged and a short-legged boy: They both were pursued from a delinquent act—the long-legged boy outran the officers and became a priest; the short-legged boy was caught, imprisoned, and became an habitual criminal.

The social environment or milieu in which we live vitally affects our personality development and adjustment. Each of us is shaped by environmental forces, many of which are subtle and unnoticed, which operate constantly and which mold us in this direction or that. No person lives in a cultural vacuum; we are largely what our culture makes us, based on how we have reacted to these cultural forces of family, community, school, friends, work environment, and leisure time or vacational pursuits; in short, we are what our previous experiences have made of us.

We are constantly acquiring what is largely a residual personality, an unconscious level of awareness, which shapes our conscious behavior in ways of which we are not aware. Modern learning theory holds that human conduct is largely the result of learned behavior; that the feedback from learning experiences is of crucial importance in a cybernetic correction and redirection of behavior, as learned reaction patterns become fixed life styles of behavior.

The so-called *intelligence* of an individual is definitely related to his chances of going to prison. The poor, unlettered, ill-dressed, unmannered, minority ethnic or racial class member is destined to comprise a disproportionate share of our prison population. It is estimated that approximately 25 percent of inmates in our prisons do not have sufficient mental ability to stay out of prison. Many are retarded, physically and/or mentally defective, illiterate or functionally illiterate (below fourth-grade levels of reading and writing), and they lack saleable job skills which could earn for them a crime-free living. They do not understand laws, are easily influenced by criminally inclined persons and cannot participate effectively in their own defense in court when under criminal trial or investigation. Such individuals are destined to be in trouble from the basic fact of their mental, emotional, and/or physical handicaps. They will continue to fill our prisons, hospitals, and relief rolls until society faces up to the need to give these handicapped and defective persons special education and job training in childhood and a sheltered environment in which they can cope throughout life. Without such training and assistance, these people will continue throughout their lives to be a costly drain on society. The question is not whether we can afford the cost of their special handling, the question is whether we can afford *not* to do it.

In the following chapters we will explore the aspects of inherited tendencies, environmental shaping, and the social factors which ultimately result in the forming of a unique personality. We will attempt to discover why one individual becomes a well-adjusted, productive citizen and another becomes a maladjusted, youthful offender—one a John F. Kennedy, the other a Lee Harvey Oswald.

Our objective will be to analyze the potent social shaping forces operating during adolescence which result in adults who are, or are not, emotionally integrated, with physical and intellectual competencies which equip them to become tax-payers rather than *tax-eaters*. We must, in fact, try to understand the adolescent animal in contemporary American society, with special reference to his special settings in the inner-city target area, which is the breeding ground for the majority of our youthful offenders. In this connection, the great power of the family to create or destroy its children in their adjustment to the realities of life will be given primary recognition: The child forecasts the man as the dawn forecasts the day, and behind each disturbed child one can find a maladjusted parent or parent surrogate (e.g., guardian, uncle).

This text is specifically intended to provide a brief and concise coverage of the essential insights which modern behavioral science has made available to assist police, corrections, and social rehabilitation students and practitioners in their increasingly frequent adversary or helping encounters with youthful offenders. The pitch of this book is that of the medical model: not to confront the *client*, or *patient*, or *respondent* with recriminations and blame; rather, to proceed in a therapeutic manner to salvage what can be saved from the threatened wreck of youthful lives as social agencies impact with the turbulence and immaturity of the adolescent years. In short, to help the officer, probationer and others involved with the manner society deals with the youth and to search for causes and possible cures instead of the details of specific acts with a view to punitive action to follow, is the goal of this book.

CHAPTER II

PSYCHOLOGY AND PHYSIOLOGY OF THE JUVENILE

E ACH CHILD AS HE matures reaches levels of development which are only incidentally related to his *Chronological Age* (C.A.). These levels or *ages* are as follows:

Mental Age (M.A.)—the *know-how* he has acquired by living in a stimulating and enriched environment or in one which is less favorable to his optimum mental maturity. This age is determined by a written test or by individual interview and performance.

Physiological Age (P.A.)—the physical maturity level reached as he lives through childhood and adolescence.

Social Age (S.A.)—the degree of social adjustment or maturity achieved from his life experience.

Emotional Age (E.A.)—the level of maturity in respect to self control, and absence of infantile temper tantrums or other childish strategies to control others.

Educational Age (Ed.A.)—the school-grade levels reached in various school subjects (not uniformly evidenced with most children).

Reading Age (R.A.)—measured by tests which show relation to reading ability norms for school grade levels.

Intelligence, defined as the ability to solve problems quickly and accurately, is measured by mental maturity tests which reveal the degree to which Thurstone's seven factors of intelligence[1] are present:

(1) Verbal comprehension (vocabulary)

(2) Word fluency

---

[1] Thurstone, L.L.: *Multiple Factor Analysis.* Chicago: University of Chicago Press, 1947.

(3) Numbers
(4) Space
(5) Memory
(6) Perception
(7) Reasoning

The scores made on these factors are related to chronological age for each individual and the result is the Intelligence Quotient (I.Q.), a ratio of mental age to chronological age. Where the M.A. is greater than the C.A., a superior mental maturity is indicated; where M.A. is less than C.A., a retarded development is shown. There are many cautions to be observed in interpreting I.Q. scores, the greatest being the influence of cultural factors which tests do not measure accurately, if at all. Another important caution is the fact that written (printed) tests require reading proficiency, which many persons do not have. Most of us read far below our potential for speed and comprehension, in part, the consequence of poor reading instruction and habits of non-reading. Almost without exception, every good reader has read a lot; every poor reader has read little. There are three ways to learn to read: read, read, and read.

The adolescent age bracket—for boys, roughly 12–17, and for girls, 10–16—is a period of marked physical developmental changes. Secondary sex characteristics mature fully by the end of this period and physical reproduction becomes possible. The changes are gradual in degree and span a period of years from onset to full development. These changes are the result of hormonal stimulation operating within the endocrine system.

Accompanying these dramatic physiological changes is a parallel emotional psychological transition from the sheltered childhood environment to the wider horizon of school and inter-personal interactions with consequent need for acquisition by each adolescent of a new set of behavioral skills in order to cope successfully with the demands for new social adjustments. The transition from childhood to adulthood is indeed a difficult period for both the adolescent and his family. Most adolescents manifest behavioral characteristics typical of the adolescent period. In fact, an adolescent who does not show most of these disturbing and, at times, bizarre characteristics to some degree at some time during his passage from childhood to adulthood would be atypical and his personality development would be most unusual. *Model* children sometimes show serious deviant behavior later in life. Parents, teachers, police, corrections and welfare workers should regard the manifestation of these, at times, troublesome behavioral patterns as normal and to be expected; instead, many adults judge adolescents by adult standards with consequent maladaptive and often harmful results for both the youths and society.

Adolescents undergo what has been called *Stürm und Drang*—storm and stress. Their personality apparently is melted down and recast anew. Old values and controls are revised and often discarded as no longer applicable. A search for a new philosophy of life, a set of values, is a formidable task for most adolescents, and this task can only be done by the person, by and for himself.

Anxiety, sometimes acutely felt, is commonplace; the external world with new compelling requirements for conformity and independence from parental controls may create grave maladjustments.

Peer group controls take precedence over parents, teachers, church and police authority. Experimentation, for example with drugs, in order not to be *chicken* is frequently reported.

Rebelliousness is commonly observed—the adolescent is testing reality by direct experience. This is a dangerous and costly process for many, but some lessons of life seemingly cannot be learned vicariously—they must be experienced at first hand. Adolescents generally are accorded a *learner's permit* status by society on the grounds that since they are not fully mature they are not to be held fully responsible for their actions. The Juvenile Court philosophy is based on this concept.

Hostility and negativism to all controls is often seen during this transition period. Reasons are asked to justify adult demands (not without justification at times) and the passive acquiescence of childhood is usually replaced by a fierce independence, a demand to be allowed to *do one's own thing,* to make one's own mistakes, if that is the result.

For a certain small percentage of adolescents, serious

deviant behavior is manifested in *acting-out* behavior, such as running away, sexual escapades, drug and alcohol abuse, and serious criminal conduct. Unconscious motivations, related to ventilation of hostility, undoubtedly operate in many such cases.

In a very small number of adolescents, full blown psychotic illness is observed. These cases must have institutional care to avoid great danger to the patient, his family and society. Prompt referral of such cases for professional medical care is imperative. The Charles Manson *family* case in California would be an example of a psychotic in need of closed-ward care.

The *school* is not responsible for all juvenile offenders, but the typical school is severely implicated in the problem. We have children with problems—not problem children. Guidance counselors are greatly needed at all school levels to help pupils resolve crisis problems of academic, personal, and social adjustments. The cost to society is great when a school fails to motivate and retain pupils until high school graduation. Some ninety percent of prison inmates are school drop-outs. Today's complex society requires that each individual be educated to the maximum of his potential for development.

For many pupils, school is an intolerable environment: they are laughed at by fellow pupils, scorned and humiliated by unprofessional teachers, and see no real benefit to their continued attendance. Society clearly must *beef up* the quality of public education for *all* the children of *all* the people, and especially for financially distressed inner-city schools (which until recent years were models of excellence in education but which now are in serious trouble as a result of indiscipline, outdated curriculum, dilapidated buildings, and inferior professional staffs in many ghetto area schools).

Parental modeling is absent or defective for many racial minority children, reaching as high as forty percent of black families in some cities. The street becomes the conditioning factor which gives anti-social conduct greater rewards than social conformity. The remarkable thing is *not* that some ten percent of ghetto residents *commit* crimes; the wonder is that ninety percent *do not succumb* to ever present temptations. For the delinquent, *the world is his oyster;* he is, in fact, adjusted—even though this involves anti-social acts.

In Freudian theory, the youthful offender shows weak or non-existent superego controls. He has not learned to have a conscience, because he was not conditioned to develop a conscience during his formative early years.

Behaviorally, the delinquent specializes in expressing his feelings overtly and in a manner that often hurts himself and others. Clinically, he has been defined as the youngster who habitually resolves his personal-social problems through overt aggressive behavior that society finds bothersome and contrary to its value identifications. For the youngster, this delinquency aggression is purposive and adjustive; from the point of view of society, it constitutes an irritating maladaptation and even full-blown crime.

Much delinquency is apparently based on what is essentially an unrecognized extension of defenses to crime in the form of justifications for deviance that are seen as valid.

The *beatniks* are mostly a protest group. They parade their nonconformity in their refusal to submit to the world of *squares.* Many live in filth; personal hygiene is completely neglected. They wear long, dirty, and uncombed hair, rarely wash themselves or the clothes they wear, and eat cold food from cans. Their attire is nondescript, and they go barefooted along the cold and filthy streets. Many wear dark glasses even at night (related to drug abuse). Their sources of money are peddling dope, prostitution, and homosexual pandering. They have a peculiar language they speak to each other. They frequent certain areas (to the disgust of the residents and the police), and live in crowded substandard rooms. Some few are arrested for burglary and housebreaking. The only skill they develop is the ability to endorse checks sent by parents happy to have them elsewhere. (One family sends checks to their son in Hawaii marked *D.C.H.*—don't come home.) The main impression these beatniks make on the police who observe them is that they are in rebellion against all social controls and against conformity. Their creed may be summarized in what they consider to be their right to *do their own thing.*

Hippies show a remarkable clannish behavior, wearing a

sort of uniform—ragged jeans and droopy shirts—with long hair, headbands, and beards, almost the passport to their midst. They do get security from identification with their peers, and their concern with anti-establishment, anti-war, anti-conglomerate monopolies, and more recently anti-pollution and consumer injustice, helps to unite them.

Many of today's typical adolescents of the ages 14 to 18 show, in varying degrees, a tendency toward alienation, a *turning off,* a refusal to become involved, a non-concerned attitude toward society at large or the establishment. This phenomenon is found among all social classes from the poorest to the most affluent, from homes where everything is lacking to homes where everything is oversupplied.

Estrangement, zealotry to the point of fanaticism, anomie (without norms or standards), bewilderment, frustration, fear, withdrawal, disengagement, indifference, apathy, neutralism, arrogance, messianic self-righteousness, extreme self-centeredness, and hostility are observed. Reckless action is justified on the grounds that individuals need not obey laws enacted by the majority (even throwing golfballs embedded with razorblades at policemen or guardsmen is not considered a criminal act in their distorted logic).

Parents are baffled by this pattern of behavior, and many despair of finding any solution until the effects of time can, hopefully, work some improvement and restore their young person to relative sanity, as the parents view it. The thousands of wandering couples to be observed on our highways and at so-called *Youth Festivals* are ample evidence of the extent of this social phenomenon. How long this counter-culture era will endure is not clear; the relative recent calm on white college campuses would appear to suggest a trend toward less militancy among youths at this time (1973). Additional descriptions of these youths might include ambivalent, splintering, decay, inhuman breakdown, disintegrated, destructive, fiercely independent, and devoted to discordant music (the nerve-wracking beat type of shrill, high decibel sounds).

In general, these youths lack enough experience of life to be able to form valid judgments relative to what is good;

they question and reject any philosophical position other than that of *Existentialism.* This view of behavior sets the individual as sole judge of his actions without regard to any authority such as family, church or moral codes. All must be decided through the funnel of self-choice. Such a position relative to life's choices presupposes a background reservoir of learning and experience which few youths possess. That many followers of this life-view have traumatic experiences as reality impacts, and that many end in disillusionment, and even suicide for some, is not surprising.

Each young person at about age twelve to fourteen must experience what is called the *existential moment,* when he realizes for the first time that he *exists,* that he cannot escape the consequences of his behavior and that significant others, such as his parents, can no longer serve to protect him from the responsibilities he must face on his own in life and from which there is no escape.

Many youths are *idealistic;* that is, they favor consumer abuse research, uplift movements, social reforms, helping the deprived and segregated, and aiding the poor and aged. These humanistic motivations are indeed noble and serve to cancel out in part the destructive anti-social actions of a minority of other youths who violently rebel against society.

Some youths show a pattern of extreme hedonism or *now-gratification,* a refusal to postpone present pleasures for later greater rewards. This present-time orientation is related to their immaturity, their lack of confidence in the stability of the future, and egocentric view of life. This attitude is often observed in ghetto youths for whom the future holds little promise as they view their present predicament, which they often term *repression.* This view is often directly related to drug abuse: the addict has lost hope of a better chance for himself, he feels boxed-in or *programmed* for a life of hardships and poverty and seeks an escape through a chemical cocoon of drugs or alcohol which shields him, at least for a few hours, from the real world which he feels he can no longer tolerate.

Negative behaviors which are characteristic of adolescents include isolation, hyperactivity, swings of mood, sex antagonisms and striving to achieve both homosexual and heterosexual identifications, daydreaming, emotional turbulence, and irritability. These all seem to peak just before full physical maturity is reached.

Adolescence is a period of emotional upheaval, of swings of moods from extreme elation to deep depression. Ambivalent feelings of love and hate are often shown toward their parents and companions. In general, much unhappiness seems the lot of many adolescents, related to their immaturity, and their adjustment is difficult and fragile for both themselves and others. This fundamental fact must be recognized by all who interact with today's adolescent.

CHAPTER III

THE FAMILY

THE TREMENDOUS influence of the home and family in shaping every child toward a satisfactory life adjustment or a collision course with disaster, cannot be overestimated. The family constellation is a most potent and subtle shaping force, with much of its effects not realized on a conscious level of recall. Here is where personality in its most plastic and malleable form is jelled, concretized, and becomes structured. It is only with great difficulty that the personality as shaped in early years (to age 4) can be remolded in later life.

The child is developing his personality from his very first breath, and the sooner the shaping forces of conformity and the development of a superego, a conscience, is performed, the better.

The human personality is today believed to be shaped by forces which may be either within or without the *psyche*—that is, human behavior is the result of learnings which are the feedback of experience as these experiences build on the genetic endowment through living. Whether one interprets the theoretical basis of behavior in terms of behaviorism (Drs. Watson and Skinner), or psychoanalytic theory (Dr. Freud), or learning theory (Drs. Dollard and Miller), or some eclectic mixture of these extremes, the fact remains that human behavior is the result of both heredity and environment as shaped by social conditioning.

Differential exposure to environmental forces is of great importance, but the genetic endowment also cannot be overlooked. We believe today that no person is *born* to be anything; he has a *potential*, which may or may not be maximally realized as his environment and his peculiar reaction to that environment determine the final product. We are, in fact, born grossly unequal; to a considerable extent our lives are *programmed* by our ancestry, and our parental socio-economic and racial circumstances, by neighborhood, schools, and non-school environment. Some accidental incidents may cause profound consequences. This is not to say that anyone is *destined* to his place in life. Each of us is today what our yesterdays made us, and will be tomorrow what our todays are making us. We grow our personalities by living them.

Each individual is believed to require the experience of *T.L.C.*—tender, loving care—for his full emotional development. The superego, or conscience, must be learned. Empathy, compassion, and social responsibility seem to be conspicuously lacking in many adolescents today who are *turned-off* from society. These seemingly cold and detached young people are believed often to have grown up where these qualities were not present in their structuring environment. The home is clearly implicated as creator of this condition. We act as we do because of feedback from our experiences, from the fallout. The technical term for this process is cybernetics. Some parents have apparently abdicated from their traditional role enactment. Children are tolerated at home as they show incorrigibility, disobedience to reasonable intra-family controls, and even drug abuse. Today one often observes an absence of parental authority, the *pater familias* concept, which has been a salient aspect in German, Italian, Greek, and Chinese immigrant first generation families during the past century in America. This breakdown of parental authority and responsibility is deplored by many sociologists; its pernicious effects are evident: physical and verbal assaults on parents, and parental discontrol, sometimes serious. Second and subsequent generations of minority families show less conformity to law-abiding behavior; San Francisco reports a recent rise in delinquency among youths of Oriental background, perhaps explained in part by the influence of non-Oriental peers and the effects of modern communications media which often negate the family and ethnic cultural patterns and values of the first generation to this country.

The family is of the utmost importance in the social conditioning process. It is the *twig-bender* whose subtle and overt effects cannot be overemphasized. The small child is, from birth, responding either favorably or unfavorably either toward or away from social adjustment, to all the input of learning from his living. These learnings have feedback corrective effects on his behavior. He will tend to repeat that behavior which is rewarding and/or satisfying and not to repeat behavior which is painful and/or unrewarding, as Professor E.L. Thorndike taught early in this century in his *theory of connectionism*. Dr. Skinner's *operant conditioning* theory, with prompt rewarding for behavior which is desired by the experimenter appears to have great potential as a device to shape mass behavior, as evidenced in Soviet Russia and Red China today and for decades past where deliberate and designed environmental conditioning is being applied to millions of humans with the announced purpose of creating a new *Socialist Man*. No input of ideas is tolerated which could possibly dilute or weaken the thinking of their citizens in exactly the direction desired. Every effort is made by all media at the government's disposal to disparage and falsify any thinking which may be *subversive* or *revisionist*. Conformity in thinking and acting is mandatory as desired by governmental authorities.

The family shapes in insidious ways, and we are not aware of the shaping which goes on very subtly, in homeopathic doses, minute portions. The family is where our attitudes are laid down. It is where we get our religious orientation, our political convictions, and develop our ideas of racism, of intolerance or of tolerance, of respect or hatred for others. It is a closed environment, at a time when the child is most plastic and receptive. He has no frame of reference to combat the ideas which are repetitively implanted day after day—not only by precept but much more effectively by examples. For example, some parents *teach* their children to kill themselves on the road by the way the parent drives: no regard for traffic laws, speeding, and reckless disregard of road courtesy—the child sees this and repeats it when he is the driver.

The parents' way of life rubs off—whether the family pays its bills or is a family of *dead-beats*, whether they are self-sufficient or are predators on the neighbors, whether the grass is cut and debris cleared away or a slum created at home.

By the time a child enters school, he is very thoroughly indoctrinated and shaped. Even four years of college changes attitudes very little in respect to racial tolerance, political bigotry, or religious orientation. Education does not necessarily erase misconceptions that are grossly untenable.

The family's closed environment during the most formative years gives the opportunity to build both conscious and unconscious value systems, a philosophy of life and style of life which is of marked permanence throughout life. The fallout from living in intimate daily interaction with parents (and here the mother's role is crucial) and significant others in the family circle, leaves permanent deep personality shapings which often manifest themselves in pathological behavior in later life. Perceptions of reality (we see things not as *they* are, but as *we* are) are clearly related to prior learnings from living.

This poses a dilemma. The family shapes us—but many times in ways that are not wholesome. Surveys indicate that while the majority of today's parents are high school graduates, we have over seventeen million Americans who are illiterate. Statistics also indicate that, generally speaking, parents who are uneducated have more children than do those who have attained a higher level of formal education. At one time in our history, a large family was thought to be the best family. Social attitudes now, however, tend to place more value on quality than on quantity. The resources of every family must be divided among the members of that family. And too often economic necessity still is one of the forces resulting in early school drop-out for the children of a large family.

That many homes are patently intolerable and unwholesome is indicated by statistics which estimate that more than one million children ran away from home in 1971 in the United States. The mother's role in the family cannot be underscored too strongly. She is the key person. Biographies of the great achievers in our society, Lincoln among them, indicate the great debt they owe to their mothers. The mother who works at the job of being a mother, offering the encouragement, the security, the smiling serenity that is priceless, has a God-given role, and the result of how effectively that role is fulfilled is largely in her hands with great consequences for society. Being a good mother, however, does not mean being an indulgent mother. It is cruelty to be over-indulgent with children, and too often is an expression not of love, but of taking the easy way out. Discipline is a basic requirement for the healthy maturation of a child's character. So-called *smother-love*, where the mother gets her emotional needs from the child, usually an only child, and where the husband is almost a non-entity, is a great threat to the child's healthy emotional maturation.

The mother who rejects her child—either consciously or unconsciously—does irreparable damage to the child. Frequently a mother rejects her child because she feels he will spoil her career by keeping her from work, or because he hampers her freedom for social activities, or simply because she is not mature enough herself to accept the responsibility of a child. She *says* that she loves the child dearly—but her actions, her body language, tells a different story. And the child senses this rejection. Even a newborn baby senses the lack of warmth, the support, the bodily fondling and caressing. Such children are often retarded in growth and show emotional difficulties very early in life, with unfavorable prognosis for good adjustment later in life.

If a mother does not really cherish her child, the child senses it. Orphanage children often show extreme emotional difficulties later in life because of the deprivation resulting from early life impersonal environment. The mother's role is to see to it that the child's physical and emotional needs are anticipated and met and that the child feels secure; the institutional environment of an orphanage rarely can provide that emotional security. Experiments in a few more progressive institutions with *substitute mothers* have been highly successful. These women, mostly volunteers, come in to the institution on a regular basis and do nothing but love and cuddle the babies, rock them, play with them, and give them the emotional warmth which the regular staff often cannot find time to do.

Child rearing practices show marked differences from culture to culture, and are believed, in Freudian theory, to have direct relationship in many cases to adult mental illness. Weaning, breast feeding, rigid toilet training, neglect, rejection, infrequent mothering, *smother-love*, corporal punishment (the battered child syndrome), the whole pattern of child care practices are of the greatest importance in personality shaping. Those children who lack the three *L's: Love, Limitations*, and *Let Them Grow Up*,[1] are likely to develop distortions of reality and possibly neurotic or even psychotic tendencies or conditions in later life. The role of the mother or the parent surrogate is crucial in the shaping of the styles of life which will be the later personality pattern of each child. The responding significant adult in interaction with the child can build security or insecurity; absence of love, confidence, and support is believed to be extremely deleterious for wholesome personality development, and this view is today given great validity by authorities in psychopathology.

Many of the ways of life and child-rearing practices commonly associated with Negro families are, in fact, more properly descriptions of lower socio-economic classes, white, black, or brown. There are high rates of broken homes (especially early desertion from family responsibilities by the father); non-concern for future contingencies of life; shifting of family care responsibilities to older siblings, grandparents, or social agencies; and minimal attention to whether the essentials of family life are adequately provided—shelter, food, economic support and emotional security. Where the family unit is a matriarchy, the boy is denied an exemplar to follow toward achieving a masculine role identity into manhood.

Parental shapings: language used, their ways of relating, the taboos which they unconsciously hold, their value systems, and role enactments and expectations, are extremely formative with their children who are in the most malleable and receptive period of their lives. These subtle influences, which are all-pervasive, are by social osmosis absorbed into the very fabric of the lives of children, without conscious

[1] Sahakian, William S.: *Psychology of Personality*. Itasca: F.E. Peacock, 1968.

awareness. We teach much more by example than by precept, and these examples transcend ethnic, religious, or social class origins.[2]

Family interaction within the family constellation is also to be considered; reciprocally inter-relating roles must be defined, with the potential ever present for distortions of reality which can be pathogenic. In the family, the basic social roles are learned, social values are defined, and the forecast for much of life's subsequent path is shaped. Infants are in fact acculturated and acclimatized, with the process largely completed by age three. Dr. Freud has always held to this theory of the enduring and often ineradicable effect of fallout from early childhood. Shapings in the family has been most fundamental to this theory of personality development and its psychopathology.

Also basic in Freudian theory is the view that early life experiences within the family constellation cannot be fully reshaped or undone. Children with severe emotional disturbances are almost without exception the product of being raised in very faulty family settings. A child's cognitive development is initiated within the family circle.

Deprivation of rich sensory input (including emotional security) during early months of life is today believed likely to jeopardize later realization of possible intellectual potential. The first eighteen months to thirty-six months of life are seen as crucial periods, when the quality of every child's mental, emotional, and physical composition is largely being firmly defined, with great possibilities for less than optimum realization being related to what occurs in the home during that time.

How the mother's role as provider of nourishment, care, and love is performed or neglected, is known to affect the intelligence, health, and maturation of all the various *ages*of the child—emotional, mental, social, and even physiological. The richness or poverty of stimulating experiences in the first few months of life are of extreme importance to optimum development. Rejection by the mother of a child's basic need for security and affection is promptly reflected in feeding

[2] Lidz, T.: *The Person*. New York: Basic Books, 1968, p. 54.

and behavioral difficulties which retard normal development of both psyche and soma. These detrimental influences are apparently in part permanent and not possible to reverse.

The father's role is not without importance, even though the mother is the key figure. The father is the male exemplar. It is he, hopefully, who gives a masculine flavor to the home, and who furnishes the stability and control which every child needs. Homosexual behavior is in large part attributed to a defective male or female model in the home.

Related to the periodic or permanent absence of the father or a male substitute in the father-role from so many homes, particularly in deprived and segregated families, many more male teachers in the elementary schools are believed to be greatly needed. The theory offered is that the masculine teacher could provide some of the pattern and the stability for the child that is lacking because of the absence of the father or a male model. The matriarch type of family (mother centered) jeopardizes the boy's role pattern achievement toward a masculine sex role in life.

The father's role as disciplinarian is one factor in the Gluecks' 5 factors[3] which predict (where all are lacking) pre-delinquency in almost every case by the age of six. The other factors are: supervision by the mother, family cohesiveness, non-submission to authority, and early evidence of destructive tendencies.

The cohesiveness or lack of it, of the family is a prime factor in the shaping of character and stable personality of a child. Excessive dependence on television for entertainment is a negative influence on family cohesiveness.

When the television is turned on, the home ceases to be a home and becomes a theater. The family does not talk; they fail to go over the events of the day; they lack support from each other; they fail to communicate. Sometimes whole evenings go by with no conversation (except during the commercials). The family turns off when the television is turned on. Television, if used judiciously, can, of course, be a source of education as well as of entertainment. But children were

---

[3] Glueck, Sheldon and Eleanor: *Predicting Delinquency and Crime.* Cambridge: Harvard University Press, 1960.

not designed to sit for hours in front of a little box. Nor should the television be used as an unpaid baby-sitter. The wise parent offers contructive occupation for a child and insists on a reasonable amount of play and exercise. *Late shows* on school nights should, of course, be out of the question. Some telecasts are clearly excellent. Excessive televiewing is a serious hazard for both the physical and mental health of many children.

Many families suffer from what has been called the *generation gap*, which is largely a communication gap. Where there is little or no interchange of ideas, feelings, or involvement between family members, when the home has no cohesiveness, where the parents do not form a workable coalition, obviously any unifying factor in the home will be small and coincidental. The television's effect as a device to mute and even destroy the family as a unit is apparent. When the family does not talk, it does not function as a family. In addition, the television media today is being questioned as to its effect on desensitizing children from the human feelings of compassion and abhorrence of violence, and the possibility of its creating distortions of reality, which, in the view of many, contributes to *sick* behavior. Reports indicate disturbed children may be greatly influenced by violence viewed on television, and recent research by the federal government indicates serious incrimination of the excessive violence shown on television is related to many children who manifest violent behavior tendencies.

It is no doubt true that *we can live through our children but not with them*. Their world is not our world, and we cannot enter it. The period of rapid social revolution we are now experiencing is evidenced by accelerated changes in dress, speech, and social conventions to a degree not believed possible in the short time since the Viet-Nam era began.

Family control *of* the child frequently, has been replaced by family control *by* the child. The young daughter does not like the piece of furniture her mother has selected, so the mother takes it back to the store. The teenage boy demands a jalopy or perhaps sports car to drive to school, and the father promptly goes out and buys one rather than fight the problem. Then the boy spends his time repairing and modifying the car—and his school work suffers. Children are very clever in bringing subtle, unremitting pressure to bear in the direction they wish in order to gain their ends. Parents are *manipulated* much more than they realize by their children, often for purposes which are undesirable for both children and parents.

In many respects, the British way of bringing up children has much to commend it—they do not *ask* a child, they *tell* him. It is well for the family to discuss the various views of family members relative to the purchase of a piece of furniture, the new car, or where to spend a vacation—and adults cannot always be presumed to be right. We must realize, however, that a child is immature, his experiential background is limited, and his judgment is therefore immature and incomplete. Thus, the final decision, the ultimate responsibility, should and must rest with the parents. Until the child reaches his maturity, parents cannot be absolved from their responsibility to hold power of final veto. Too often, parents buy a motorcycle as the *last present* for a son, on his sixteenth birthday. In their later sorrow they realize that it was indeed a *last* present—from anyone. The number of fatal and permanent disability (amputations) accidents in which motorcycles are involved has increased during the past five years to an alarming degree. They might even properly be called *murder* cycles.

The family may reflect a culture of poverty—or a poverty of culture. Poverty as a way of life is the life program which thousands of inner-city families manifest. Here the vicious circle of the *un-people* is readily observed: *un*education leads to *un*employment, to *un*healthy housing and diet, and *un*desirable citizenship (subsisting on relief, and hospital charity).

A society which perpetuates a culture of poverty is in part responsible for this triad of poverty, crime, and punishment (which not only does not rehabilitate, but instead almost always brutalizes and alienates offenders against society). Punishment will be the topic of a later chapter.

Siblings in the family exert a great influence on each other.

Birth order is receiving more attention as a personality shaper, with the first-born apparently becoming, generally, the most successful in life. Rivalries, jealousies, and mutual helpfulness are all possible and their mixes in daily family interaction are significant in personality determinations.

The psychoanalytic view of the family as a pathogenic factor is undoubtedly important in mental illness. No family can expect to create an ideal environment; traumatic experiences will certainly occur—death, long separation from a parent (as, for example, required by military service), economic crises—and these will leave permanent emotional scars. At the same time, the family can be a foundation for emotional equilibrium and behavioral stability. The almost total absence of adolescent criminal behavior in first generation Chinese-American families and in Jewish families in the United States is proof of the great control that family cohesiveness can exert.

Family disorganization, disintegration, and psychopathology is commonly observed today. Some claim that three-fourths of all marriages are failures. The divorce rate of one in three marriages is serious indicator of possible breakdown of the family in our society. The unfortunate consequences for children of broken homes needs no elaboration. The stresses of urban living are great even with both parents present; when one parent only or the grandparents must do the job, conditions for psychopathology are more likely to be present.

The goal of every nuclear family should be to raise children who will be emancipated from dependency on the parents. This means that support and subsidy for even a long educational period (a legitimate and proper use of family resources) is to be distinguished from continued dependency for *hippie* living, drug abuse, and student revolutionary activity. Parental toleration and coddling of adolescent and post-adolescent idleness and debauchery is impossible to reconcile with responsible parenthood. It is as cruel to distort reality for adolescents by overprotection and overindulgence as to fail to support them in a school or job training.

The golden Grecian mean of moderation between neglect and overprotection is difficult to achieve. Perhaps if more errors were made on the side of too early requirement of self-support for adolescents, there would be less trouble. Affluence, providing access to automoblies, liberal spending money, mobility to travel long distances by automobile or air (often on weekends when work or college study is neglected), and tendency on the part of many overprotected youths to avoid work—these are definitely related to the social malaise from which many youths suffer today. These same overindulged youths are prone to criticize *the establishment* and blame their parents and society for their personal alienation and unhappiness.

The family as an economic interdependent entity is rarely found today. The old Russian proverb to the effect that *labor is the house that love lives in,* is applicable to few families today. Apartment living, early family separation for school and work, and the total absence of work chores at home, preclude achievement of the wholesome effects of group endeavor. The rural atmosphere of earlier days where all members of a family, of necessity, shared in the tasks and each member contributed to the very survival of the family resulted in family cohesiveness which has, unfortunately, deteriorated to an alarming degree as urbanization has advanced.

Another factor noted in studies of disturbed children is the apparent increasing incidence of emotional maladjustment in the parents. Behind every disturbed child can usually be found a disturbed adult. Parents with marginal emotional adjustments and/or serious borderline psychotic states are unsuitable to guide children. Most psychiatrists agree that schizophrenia is *home grown* in a social climate of stress and uncertain expectations for conformity on the part of the child. Pill-taking parents often have drug-abusing children. Early diagnosis of incipient mental illness and prompt treatment at this stage is imperatively needed by many maladjusted parents who show various early warnings of personality disintegration such as alcoholism, drug abuse, sexual maladjustment, and work absence or job dissatisfaction.

Suicide, the most frequent cause of death at age fifteen, always has a preceding history which should alert the family of impending danger. All parents would be well advised to listen to their children, to the subtle cries for help they show. The deep depression, anxiety, and extreme swings of mood which some adolescents evidence should be taken seriously and the child referred for medical and psychiatric help as promptly as possible. Frequently these distress signals may be noted by school teachers or counselors even before they become evident to the parents and should certainly be brought to the attention of the parents.Unfortuately, many of these indications of serious emotional breakdown are not taken seriously by the associates of the sick person. It is evident that many parents are completely deceived by their children who are on hard drugs; a fatal overdose may be the first warning signal some parents receive.

While the most common failure of parents is inattention or lack of concern for adolescent problems, there are, according to Professor D. Levy, M.D.,[4] four basic indices of parental overprotection (which he calls *smother love*):

1. Excessive contact of the mother with the adolescent;
2. Prolongation of services rendered customarily to very young children;
3. Prevention of development of individual behavior; and
4. Overcontrol (excess maternal control).

One of the best known authorities in the area of adolescent psychology, Dr. Kenneth Kenniston, has described the process of identity formation, which the family helps to define, as follows:

> The achievement of identity requires in every person an implicit set of goals and standards—usually those provided by society—which tell him who he is, where he stands, whence he comes, and whither he goes. . . . The price paid for opposition to society is inner convulsion, disunity, and fragmentation.[5]

All families experience ambivalent feelings of love and hate. The same father who can buy a new automobile for a son or daughter must, at times, take away the keys as a result of improper use of that car. Parental abdication of their inescapable role incumbency, however, is deplorable. The

[4] Levy, D.M.: *Material Overprotection*. New York: Columbia University Press, 1943.

[5] Kenniston, K.: *The Uncommitted: Alienated Youth in American Society*. New York: Harcourt, Brace & World, 1965, pp. 184–187.

family as a viable social organism is threatened today. Let us hope its defects are corrected before we see the family disintegrate as an institution.

Lidz, an authority on psychiatric aspects of family life, writes in connection with parental responsibility:[6]

> The family and the child rearing it provides obviously also vary with the personalities of the parents; and how the child's enculturation is carried out depends greatly upon how the parents grew up and internalized the societal patterns and the culture which became part of their personalities. They transmit the cultural ways to their offspring through the language they use, their ways of relating, the taboos which they unconsciously hold, their value systems, and their role assumptions and expectations more than through what they consciously teach to their children. Differences reflecting the individuality of the parents and how they interrelate transcend ethnic, religious, and social class origins.

This observation epitomizes the thrust of this chapter in its recognition of the salient power of the family to mold socially adjusted children, or regrettably, to produce depraved and degenerate predators on society. Each child is an omnibus in which all of his life experiences and ancestry ride, and which each day is reshaped to cope with life, for better or worse, by living experiences.

[6] Lidz, Theodore: *op. cit.* p. 54.

CHAPTER IV

THE PEER GROUP

THE FAMILY constellation is the setting for the intra-family turmoil manifested in the hostility, the difficulties, and in the lack of cohesiveness of many families. However, the family constellation is not the entire social milieu of our adolescents; for some it is the weakest influence in later years of this period. School, peer groups, the neighborhood, and organized social agencies, such as the YMCA, Boy Scouts, Girl Reserves, church, and, regrettably, delinquent gangs also may shape in part this course of development.

Probably the most potent control over an adolescent is his peer group: only a very brave youth will deviate from the norms of his own fellows. This subtle control is pervasive and thorough; it operates on both conscious and unconscious levels; moreover, it is especially powerful during the late adolescent years.

The word *peer* means an equal, or one having approximately the same age, education, and social standing. A high school graduating class is considered a peer group. The class of a military academy is a peer group. A group of army or navy recruits, or a police academy class, where they may or may not be in residence in barracks yet really get to know the characteristics of each of their colleagues, is a peer group. An additional important consideration is the power of the group in creating a group consensus, which sets standards of behavior and values, and compels compliance.

Part of the explanation of peer group control is the psychological defense mechanism of identification. The individual feels insignificant and powerless, but by joining with his peers he shares a sense of their collective power.

33

If this power is shown in mass action—such as a protest march—there is a feedback to strengthen his feeling of belonging. When he wears a costume similar to others, he feels identification; his own weakness is lessened and he may even feel omnipotent, as do mob members.

Another explanation—also a defense mechanism—is projection. The individual feels his deficiencies, but by blaming others, as in a bigoted racist group, for even more serious defects, he is able to minimize his own faults in his own eyes. Hence, he feels less insignificant and better adjusted. However, when there is systematic or prolonged reliance on both identification and projection, incipient mental illness may be present.

The peer group sets standards of conformity which apparently derive from mass consensus and follow-the-leadership of some exemplar—a charismatic or personable individual who is accepted by the group as arbiter and authority. This leader may be a star athlete, physically attractive, or it may be a *freak*, such as Charles Manson, who sets his own peculiar requirements for members of his *family*, and who compels absolute conformity. In any event, the peer group results in a relatively homogenous closed circle of in-group members who show solidarity and give group support to members. The police as an organization show marked adherence to peer group controls. This may or may not be beneficial to society at large.

Children in play groups both fear and obey; they are fear-controlled from the first time they are placed with other children. The most frequent behavior patterns are accepted and it takes a courageous child to deviate in any way from this pattern. Modern psychology plays down fear as a desirable form of social control; prompt reward for desired behavior (Dr. Skinner's Reinforcement Theory) is much preferred (See Chapter XI).

The *flower children* (or *freaks* as they are currently being called) are an example of a peer group in operation. The first characteristic of this *hang loose* culture is the *uniform*—bare feet or moccasins, ragged clothing, headband, beads, uncombed hair, sloppy attitude, and absence of personal hygiene. Not all persons who go barefoot can be called *freaks,* of course, but it is one thing to walk on nicely mowed grass and then come in and wash your feet in a sterile solution, and quite another thing to walk along filthy city streets barefooted and neglect to wash the feet for days on end. These counter-culture types are exposed to skin infections, rheumatic fever, hookworm infestation, pediculosis, malnutrition, neglect of dental hygiene and epidemic social diseases in their midst.

Today's youth in its extreme swings of mood seems almost psychotic—that is, out of touch with reality. Unreasonable demands are made for early total freedom from personal responsibility for behavior which may even be criminal in nature—such as drug abuse, arson, and throwing stones at police and national guardsmen. Youths plead that they have the *right* to *do their own thing,* without regard to the social or personal consequences of their deviant behavior. It is true that their behavior is judged to be deviant by the *square* or *straight* adult society; however, without the labor and organization of this *square world,* these youths would not be clothed or fed. Their behavior is *criminal* when they violate laws and harm the person and property of others; their adolescent status is clearly no excuse for felonious and heinous acts.

When groups of peers meet and rationalize—*rapping* is their word for it—they seemingly are able to convince each other of the propriety and legitimacy of their decisions, and numbers of youths conform to the way of life of the *freaks,* with their style of dress and non-conforming life (drop out from school, avoid work except in extreme need, and violent support for any and all *liberal* social issues, such as defense of the Attica inmates).

One must hasten to recognize that the deviants to whom we refer in the foregoing paragraphs represent less than one percent of the total youth population. The great mass are attending schools and/or working with dedication. Those who show deviant behavior, however, are vocal and visible. More than seven and one-half million American youths are in our colleges, pursuing vocational goals today and are not attracting attention by exotic behavior; the small visible minority of youthful dissidents create a false impression of today's youth.

The youthful offender shows the negative attributes to a more pronounced degree than the youthful nonoffender, and in addition he *acts out* his unconscious motivations; he shows marked impairment of ego control; his ability to adjust his gratification to reality is minimal. He acts often on impulse at the moment, with little or no conception of the consequence of his acts. He wants his gratifications now, not in an uncertain future.

Many youthful offenders have been conditioned by the feedback effects of their anti-social life cycle to respond negatively to usual social controls. Many have found that they win by delinquent acts oftener than they lose and are punished. This finding must, of course, reinforce their sociopathic behavior. Too often, deviate behavior is rewarded (as evidenced by the position of leadership granted to the *outlaw* or the misfit by many youth groups), and socially desirable behavior may not be reinforced, and even perhaps discouraged. This may well be attributed in part to the vicarious sense of fulfillment derived by the members of the *herd* when the leader does that which the individual youths do not quite dare to do alone. Mob hysteria has long been recognized as a powerful force in criminal acts.

Gang affiliation is still a serious police problem in inner city areas. The gangs survive year after year with new leadership and recruited members. The leaders are described as possessing considerable leadership ability and their continued position as leader depends on their judgment and authority. Some of these gangs in recent years have become extremely vicious; homicides are frequently reported from their *rumbles,* in contrast to a generation ago when fists were used instead of zip guns or knives. Drug abuse is related to gang behavior, with some gangs fighting against drug addiction, and deposing leaders who become addicts. Discipline is strictly maintained by the leader. The common view of gang members appears to be a conviction that their conduct is right because it is held to be wrong by the larger society around them. The following quotation from Thrasher, written two generations ago, applies equally to today's gang member:

> He breaks up a party, molests school children, taunts women and
> girls on the streets, engages in petty thievery of personal belongings.
> He is a vandal. It gives him pleasure to despoil and destroy property
> wherever the opportunity arises. He does not hold a job. Being
> a loafer, he is often found on the streets or in poolrooms. He idles
> away countless hours in smoking, gambling, and rough horseplay.
> He is always ready to foment a brawl but seldom willing to engage
> in a fair fight unless backed by his pals. He is coarse and vulgar
> in his talk. In totality, he is a thoroughly disorganized person.[1]

This is the hoodlum. He is a young member of a gang
whose demoralizing influence easily promotes criminal
behavior. However, if he remains with the gang and the process is not checked, the end product will inevitably be a
seasoned gangster or professional criminal.

Peer group controls are a phenomenon. Suffice it to say
that most young people today are not particularly fearful of
parental approval, or that of the clergy, the police, or of the
school authorities. College students often are not afraid of
deans—but they surely are afraid of those in their immediate
entourage, those with whom they associate. It is characteristic
of the young to conform, to avoid any unusual dress or
behavior, and to guard against any deviation which may earn
them the label of *chicken.*

The milieu in which a youth moves, his peer group
affiliation, is a potent shaper of his philosophy of life, his
school relationship, and his conformity (or nonconformity)
to the expectations of family and society. Differential opportunity to be exposed to influences which lead to integration
of his personality or to its disintegration, shape the individual
to a marked degree. The kind of peers he associates with
—whether they are freaks, anti-social, and even delinquent,
or *straights,* who are upward mobile and accept deferred
gratifications to achieve a future goal—is believed to be highly
significant. Parental pressures on youths to change peer group
membership is often futile; environmental manipulation,
where possible, is one partial solution in some cases.

---

[1] Thrasher, Frederic M: "The gang." *Juvenile Delinquency.* Edited by Richard
R. Korn. New York, Thomas Y. Crowell Co., 1968 p. 66.

Some neighborhoods are considered to have ten times as much exposure to delinquency generating influences as others. If the non-school hours are shaped by gang activities, if the street is the milieu, one can reasonably expect the learning feedback to be less than ideal. Many thousands of youths who have dropped out of school, who are unemployed (and this is many times higher for nonwhites than for whites), and who see around them exemplars who have *made it*— criminals, drug pushers, and deviates—are led to believe and accept as fact that *crime pays*.

For college youths, fraternities and sororities offer *in-group* status and self-esteem to the members. These *Greek* societies are not without negative aspects on college campuses, however. There is a great deal of rivalry among the groups, and the lines of social class distinction are perhaps nowhere as finely drawn as they are among the various fraternities and sororities. Academic excellence is a fraternity goal on many campuses, and the experience of living in a peer group has values which may and do contribute to success in later life.

Another phenomenon of the counterculture has been the so-called youth ghettoes, for example, at Berkeley, California. Large numbers of drop-outs, students, anti-establishment graduates, and more transient *street people* have been gravitating into segregated (youths only) communes. Here they feel comfortable with their long-haired, easy-going, *hang-loose* peers. Others, such as AWOL's, runaways, and drug addicts also live there as a last resort to hide or seek aid or shelter. Free medical attention is often available at a community clinic staffed by volunteers. Two goals appear to attract youths to these collectives: to overcome isolation and to gain solidarity. Some commune members are militants, some *peaceniks*, some drug freaks. The commune is an enclave in which only certain laws are enforced, and only certain styles of living are acceptable. *Ripping-off* (stealing) is rampant and has caused commune cooperative stores to fail. The goal of these communal settings apparently is to break down *privitization*, and to create cooperative neighborhoods. The viability of these youth ghettoes is fragile and many fail, notably one in Madison, Wisconsin.

The youth unconventional sub-culture provides group sanction, symbols, and support for the way of life which has become common for thousands of non-conforming youths, not only in the United States but world-wide. Notable exceptions are Soviet Russia and Red China, where such freedoms do not exist. Thanks to parental subsidies and society's permissiveness, today's social revolution has succeeded in changing the very fabric of our society. The velocity of social change, as shown in dress, attitudes, and social values, is a fact of life today.

Representative of the drastic changes in society are the voting privileges in local elections extended in some states to the 18–21 year old group; extreme styles of clothing (or lack of it); revised (and perhaps abandoned by some) sexual standards; and more license in speech, movies, television, and the press—actually bordering at times on hard core pornography. There is little doubt, too, that youth protest has affected national politics to a marked extent, with major political parties making an all-out effort to win votes of youths.

Many have observed that some of the goals of today's youth are indeed laudable and proper: the fight against consumer abuses, the war against pollution, the spotlighting of the anonymity and powerlessness of the individual when confronted by the great monopolistic corporations, the protest against the war in Viet-Nam (which strangely omits mention of the invasion of South Viet-Nam or atrocities by the Viet-Cong), disapproval of the extinction of wild life and abuses of conservation, less materialistic goals, concern for the poor, and the expressed horror concerning man's inhumanity to man. These idealistic youth have been called *forerunners*—with a new set of values that put social contribution and meaningful work (contrasted to assembly-line depersonalization) ahead of income, success, and security. These youths are restless, mobile, demanding, frequently absent, turbulent, resentful of job discipline, and feel a sense of personal irrelevance in a technological era.

Charles A. Reich's *The Greening of America* contends that *new ways of thinking and living—long hair, student protest, rock music, rejection of old careers* represent a *revolution by consciousness* that will save American society from dehumanization at the hands of the corporate state.

The primary objection of the critics of today's youth is not necessarily to its goals, but rather to its method of achieving those goals.

That youths do not coincide in their views with the older generations (twenty years is considered a generation) is not new to the world; that youths can effect the far-reaching changes which have occurred in recent years, is new. The political *clout* of the 18–21 year old voters can be significant, especially in local elections where large student populations may out-number permanent residents.

Peer group control is not, of course, limited to the young. We have peer control in our standards of personal hygiene. In the United States we have a generally higher standard of personal hygiene than in most developing countries around the world. Only ten percent of the Russian people have access to flush toilets. To most of the people in the world, the sanitary way of life is almost unknown. In some Asian countries, all running water is believed to be pure. There it is not uncommon to have toilets emptying into a stream while downstream that same water is used by people for drinking and to wash their dishes and clothing; soap is almost non-existent; scalding water is rarely to be found; potable water itself is in short supply. But most of the people have the same standards for that particular area. *That* is peer control, just as the peer control that requires youths in a certain group to wear fringed blue jeans, beads, headbands, to smoke marijuana, or to have a *beer-bust* every Friday night. The difference is that youth has not attained the judgment or the experience or the confidence of self to vary from the norm—even in its own best interests.

In conclusion, the power of the peer group is impossible to underscore too heavily; it is relatively independent of parental, school, police or church control; it is highly flexible and unstable; it must be recognized for what it is: a phenomenon of today's social revolution which must be respected and its effects at least recognized and hopefully understood by all who interact with youths. To this end, encounter groups (rap sessions) for parents and children, and students and college authorities, can help sensitize both youths and adults to some of the problems of adolescents. Such communication channels should hopefully have been open from early childhood. There is a patent need for programs on how to be a parent. The consequences for failure of adults to relate meaningfully with today's youths could be disastrous to the perpetuation of society as we now know it. Clearly, today's youths will be tomorrow's adults and *power* figures.

An experienced police officer has commented relative to changes in his personal attitudes as a result of this course and text: "I have come to understand especially in the chapter about peer groups why my sons wear their hair longer than I like it. I can also now understand that the snarling, spitting, sneering youth is emitting signs that delve far deeper into societal problems we adults face and have to cope with than his dislike for me as a person and as an officer."

CHAPTER V

HETEROSEXUAL AND HOMOSEXUAL RELATIONS

SEXUAL BEHAVIOR and its many social manifestations is a pervasive and powerful force for both healthy personality shaping and its disintegration. The intimacy of sexual outlet forms causes it to be a fruitful source of deep emotional turmoil and maladjustment. No other form of human behavior is as vulnerable to defective expression as is sex.

Dr. Freud placed sexual motivations as a key factor in his psychoanalytic theory. In brief, he believed that personality development and efficient human behavior throughout life were dependent on resolution of powerful instinctual sexual drives and their later-life expression in socially desirable forms. To him, the human animal was primarily moved in behavior by sexually-related deep personality factors which were formed and structured by both genetic and environmental forces, and largely were the result of very early life experiences centering upon relationships with parental figures (his Oedipus and Electra complexes). Infantile sexuality was the source of conflicts and neuroses, in Freud's opinion.

There is ample evidence today that sexual themes dominate advertising, drama, speech, films, television, styles of dress; the *pitch* of motor vehicle sales (a girl draped over the hood of a convertible) clearly proves this point. We are indeed living in a sexual revolution: books, films, magazines, and television have had almost complete relaxation of the censorship standards prevalent as recently as five years ago. Dress styles and colors reflect this change; perhaps the word *psychodelic* (or mind-altering) best describes these changes we all notice around us.

42

Adolescents are approaching the peak of sexual potency and these hormonal drives have great physiologic force. These motivations contribute greatly to the storm and stress of the adolescent years. An adjustment involving socially approved satisfactions of these powerful drives must be somehow achieved, or their expression in serious anti-social behavior will almost certainly result.

For some adolescents this process ends in failure to reach orthodox typical heterosexual identifications and relationships. These cases we label deviates or perverts, yet their form of sexual outlet may, for them, be satisfactory and rewarding. Recent social rethinking relative to unorthodox sexual outlets is in the direction of more tolerance (for example, homosexual relations between consenting adults in private is not a crime in England nor in several states in the United States of America).

Heterosexual adjustments are a form of learned behavior. Where the environmental shapings have been distorted by parental modeling, learnings from the peer group, and/or institutional living (e.g., prisons), the result is observed to be a much greater incidence of homosexual outlets. It is the considered view of most authorities that homosexual behavior is almost entirely learned and is almost never genetically determined. Some homosexuals can be *conditioned* to a heterosexual pattern; however, others do not appear to want or to be capable of changing. The life space of homosexuals is not usually conducive to their continued happiness: jealousy, fleeting liaisons, absence of a cohesive family relationship, and even violence, are often noted, with poor prognosis for later-life interpersonal adjustment. The condition is diagnosed, as are other forms of sexual perversion, as evidence of gross ego failure; the pervert is unable to relate satisfactorily to orthodox heterosexual outlets.

It is believed that homosexual behavior is largely the product of parental shaping: the boy has no real mother to relate to and the girl has no real father figure to help set her life pattern. In addition, the learnings in a homosexual environment reinforce latent unconscious homosexual drives which most individuals possess without awareness on a conscious level. The resolution of the *Oedipal complex* is essential for wholesome heterosexual pattern formation. Lasting heterosexual adjustments are very difficult to achieve for many couples. As stated above, the degree of intimacy and emotional involvement is extreme in sexual relations. The delicate balance of psychological and physiological factors required makes maladjustment of sexual outlets most difficult to avoid. When immaturity and emotional blocks, such as from frigidity and impotence, are present, serious consequences involving incompatability and hostility are sure to be present. Some estimates set the proportion of *marriage busts* at 75 percent, in terms of lasting mutual sexual satisfaction.

The psychopathic deviations of sexual outlets, such as forced perversions and criminal assaults, clearly involve degrees of mental illness and should be regarded as belonging in a medical (psychiatric) context, and not, as is usually done, in a criminal or court setting. Criminal behavior may well be involved; however, the *sickness* of the accused is a fact which must be recognized. Some psychotic sexual deviates may be potentially dangerous and some should doubtless be confined for life; others may, with psychiatric help, be restored to society and become taxpayers rather than *tax-eaters*. Early indications of serious sexual deviations among adolescents should clearly be regarded as warning signals, and prompt referral for psychiatric help is imperative. Early treatment of all mental illness, including sexual deviancy, is extremely important; such cases do not get better spontaneously; on the contrary, they almost always get worse if permitted to continue untreated. Psychosis is loss of contact with reality, and closed-ward care in maximum security is indicated for such patients.

The need for early (junior high school is too late) sex education is obvious, as evidenced by junior high school pregnancies, the epidemic rates of venereal diseases, ignorance of facts of basic physiology, and divorce rates running about one in three marriages. Many juvenile-age marriages are highly vulnerable to failure, related directly to the psychological immaturity of the couple. The tragedy is that basic ignorance of physical and psychological facts is often the direct cause of marital incompatibility and unhappiness. Inadequacies of sexual performances are rarely physical; the trouble is not from the neck down, it is from the neck up.

Sexual promiscuity is often related to *acting-out* behavior. The girl or boy is ventilating hostility against parents or society; the boy wants to *prove* his masculinity by fathering a child; the girl seeks popularity, or money and clothes otherwise denied. Such unconscious motivations are most often found in immature, insecure, distorted, and neglected home environments.

The peer group is a potent shaping force, as already discussed. Where parents are unable to relate meaningfully to their children, for whatever causes, sexual deviations from societal norms often are evidenced. Where the home does not reflect mutual respect and a coalition between husband and wife, where fighting and violence are often present, deviate behavior is the norm for the children in that home. There is little doubt that the *hippie* culture is based on the satisfactions which members get from sexual freedom, drug abuse, and belonging to a peer group (a sense of family) which they did not get, or *thought* was lacking, in their home setting.

It is estimated that some four to eight percent of males and perhaps two percent of females are predominately homosexual; some of these are bisexual, with both male and female partners at times. These high percentages mean that there are millions of homosexuals in every country. Some relation of homosexual behavior and crime exists, with cases of homicide and blackmail often not reported. In general, homosexuals are not inclined to use violence. Their activities seldom come to police attention, for obvious reasons: their activities are *no-victim,* interpersonal relations—unless minors are involved or force or threats are used.

The relationship of prostitution to drug abuse is well known. Some four hundred to five hundred dollars a week is needed to support a heroin addict; to get this much money by working is not possible for addicts—crime must be the solution for them. The pitiful cases of addicted prostitutes are shocking. Children born of addicted mothers are born with physical addiction. The percentage of drug addicts who successfully quit the habit is estimated to be less than one percent.

The Kinsey Reports of the mid-1950's drew back the curtain

on the American bedroom. The ten thousand cases of both male and female respondents revealed many startling and hitherto unknown facts relative to human sexual behavior.[1] Difference in types, frequency, and psychological factors in sexual outlets were identified for social classes. Subsequent research studies have shed additional needed light on this extremely important aspect of human behavior, with research currently being continued.

For many adolescents, the formative years are a cruel jungle of rating and dating, cars, clothing, athletic competition (to make the team), scholastic stress (for college eligibility), and attempts to remain a member of the *in-crowd*.

Some parents pressure their children into early dating and adult-type social relationships. This forced *hot-house* environment is doubtless hazardous for many children, particularly as it relates to sexual aspects of immaturity.

That adolescent sexual behavior is fraught with hazards for both sexes is clearly evident. Tragedies of extra-marital pregnancies, venereal diseases, abortions, and related suicides are commonly reported. Sex is a force of the most violent power; to fail to give sexual motivation its due is to deny reality. A rational understanding of the role of sex in contemporary American life is imperative for all. Dr. Freud's creative genius has indicated the tremendous and pervasive scope of human sexuality. The validity of his views in this connection cannot be denied today. A frank acceptance of this fact is needed, together with education to unmask ignorance concerning sex.

Seventy percent of venereal cases are in the fifteen to twenty-five year age bracket, and half of all venereal cases occur among homosexuals, according to 1972 estimates by epidemiologists who have access to fairly accurate data.

Full-blown epidemic venereal diseases are rampant worldwide today, with the youth counter-culture particularly vulnerable and infected. Ignorance and misinformation is a shocking aspect of this grave threat to the nation's health

---

[1]Kinsey, A.C., Pomeroy, W.B., and Martin, C.E.: *Sexual Behavior in the Human Male*. Philadelphia: Saunders, 1948; and Kinsey, A.C., Pomeroy, W.B., and Martin, C.E.: *Sexual Behavior in the Human Female*. Philadelphia: Saunders, 1953.

and well-being. The irreversible consequences of untreated syphillis and gonorrhea are debility and invalidism and include sterility, blindness, psychopathy, and early death.

That today's youths hold many distorted ideas relative to VD is obvious; abysmal ignorance of the physiology, psychology and biology of the venereal diseases are, together with similar ignorance concerning drug abuse, major tragedies afflicting youth. Knowledge taught by schools during late grammar years and early junior high school years is imperatively needed. Unfortunately, misguided parents and school authorities often fail to see the great need for sex education, sex hygiene, and family planning instruction. The consequences of such ignorance is catastrophic for many young victims.

The question relative to the origins of homosexual behavior, whether it is a product of faulty biology or is the result of sexual socialization cannot be answered definitively; doubtless both nature (genetic endowment) and nurture (environmental shapings) operate in unknown proportions with any individual's development. We are each of us the product of heredity and environment as shaped by social conditioning.

Theories which attribute homosexual behavior to environmental shapings point to family settings in which individuals develop incapacitating fears of the opposite sex and kindred characteristics conducive to homosexual tendencies. Life histories of many homosexuals show similar shaping forces, with certain kinds of sexual socialization inordinately common: maternal domination, with a close-binding intimate (CBI)[2] mother who accorded them preferential treatment. Many mothers were overcontrolling in their dealings with their sons, behaved seductively toward their sons, overstimulated their sons sexually within the context of an overclose, overintimate relationship, and at the same time, through antisexual attitudes, prohibitions, and demasculinizing behavior toward their sons, compelled them to conceal all manifestations of sexuality. The sons were in a double bind of maternal seductiveness and maternal sexual restrictions. The fathers of most

[2] Gibbons, Don C.: *Society, Crime and Criminal Careers.* Englewood Cliffs: Prentice-Hall, 1968, p. 402.

homosexuals were detached, hostile, and openly rejecting figures, dominated by the mother. The child cannot relate to the parents in their proper gender role, and tends to turn to the mother for guidance and to see the father as weak.

It is probable that homosexual behavior is related to hidden but incapacitating fears of the opposite sex. Unconscious motivations clearly play a large part in the homosexual syndrome of both male and female deviants.

Female deviants are usually from families dominated by repressive, authoritarian mothers who were sexually anxious while their fathers were physically punitive. Homosexuals are usually from disordered families, and begin their homosexual activities at an early age.

Kallman's research as reported in Brody[3] would lend credence to the genotype theory. He found that among hard-core homosexuals who were frequently reported to him by various agencies, that there was 100 per cent concordance rates among a group of thirty-seven male identical twins, while the concordance rate was only twelve per cent among twenty-six male fraternal twins.

Freud tended to explain problems of homosexuality through recourse to an innate bisexuality in all organisms, pointing out that the male and female sex organs differentiate from the same embryonic rudiments.

It is not believed today that an extra X or Y chromosome is, in itself, an explanation for homosexual behavior. Many individuals possess this extra chromosome and yet they live in heterosexual adjustment. Lidz[4] cites evidence which indicates that because of prenatal genetic and hormonal influences, humans are disposed at birth to a male or female gender orientation, but that such influences only predispose to a pattern that can be modified greatly by subsequent life experiences.

Clearly contingent or non-contingent reinforcement by feed-back cybernetic (circular causal chains from which goal-seeking and self-controlling forms of behavior emerge) effects from life's experiences are related to all human behavioral

[3] Brody, Nathan: *Personality* New York, Academic Press, 1972, p. 169.
[4] Lidz, T.: op. cit, p. 210.

patterns, such as alcoholism, drug addiction, fetishism, enuresis, transvestism, obesity, psychopathic and criminal behavior, and including homosexuality. Apparently a failure of proper conditioning has occurred.

Aversion therapy using pictures, slides, electric shocks, have been successful in changing some homosexuals to heterosexual patterns. Some individuals are intermittently bisexual, with partners of either sex preferred at times.

Recently militant homosexuals have struck out at the discrimination, humiliations, punishment and harrassment of which many people express toward homosexuals. These militants allege that society is wrong in forcing homosexuals into the role of an oppressed minority. This makes the homosexual a revolutionary, along with oppressed and militant groups like blacks and women. They say homosexuality is assuredly no advantage, but it is nothing to be ashamed of, no vice, no degradation, it cannot be considered an illness. They consider it to be a variation of sexual functions produced by a certain arrest of sexual development. Zero population growth is, of course, aided by homosexuals.

CHAPTER VI

THE JUVENILE COURT THEORY

Two BASIC CONSIDERATIONS must underlie this review of the juvenile court: one, the need for a philosophy or theory of a separate, civil, non-punitive agency of society for adjudication of juvenile anti-social acts or acts of society against juveniles (such as neglect or abuse of children of tender ages); and, two, that this need has been met in only a small proportion of cases of juveniles who are referred for judicial disposition of difficulties which confront youths as adversaries with the law, or as persons who need protection by the law (neglected children).

The *dream* has been for a separate court whose sole reason for existence is the hope that it can salvage something from the anti-social predicaments in which almost half of all children find themselves at one or more times during their adolescent years. The idea of any *punishment* for violations of law is inappropriate and contradictory to the spirit of such a court. There is a *respondent*, not a *defendant*. Due process protection of the juvenile is to be the same as for adults. The proceedings are of civil, not criminal nature. The purpose is to *rehabilitate*, to *re-educate*, to *protect*, and to *reintegrate* the respondent into trouble-free life in open society. No stigma or permanent *record* is to be attached to juveniles which will be a handicap throughout later life, prejudicing employment, exclusion from many professions, and jeopardizing a crime-free adult life.

Central to this theory is the view that juveniles (to age eighteen, or in some states to twenty-one) are not fully mature, and hence are not to be held fully responsible for their behavior which deviates from social norms. A *learning permit* idea is to be kept in mind. This is not to exculpate or mitigate the seriousness of juvenile misdeeds (the victim of these acts is just as dead or injured as if it were the act of an adult); however, because of the tender years and immature judgment of the juvenile offender, the juvenile court is to view his acts in a different light from that of the older offender. This light is characterized by a belief that there is nothing to be gained by punishment; rather, all may be lost by it. The anti-social acts of children should be regarded more as behavior problems, than as criminal acts.

Confinement as therapy is semantic acrobatics. However, it must be accepted that some juveniles must be confined for their own safety and that of society; for example, individuals not treatable in the open society because of severe mental illness involving departure from reality. Others must be removed from open society for short periods in order to correct distortions of reality, and, hopefully, to instill social habits of conformity based on the operant conditioning theory, in which the consequences of behavior are promptly rewarded when they are socially desirable and behavior which is anti-social is ignored or punished.[1] In this connection, a few experimental programs are in operation, notably at the Robert F. Kennedy Center, Morgantown, West Virginia, where a token economy operates to redirect behavior by operant conditioning. The success or failure of this idea is not yet possible to assess.

The late Director J. Edgar Hoover of the Federal Bureau of Investigation has characterized one view of juvenile behavior:

> A segment of our society has offered all types of excuses and rationalizations: unhappy childhood, lack of opportunity, emotional stress, influence of narcotics or alcohol—but they seem never to consider that some of these punks are plain mean.

Another view would be that all behavior is the result of learning, and that the feedback from life experiences shapes behavior in directions which are either socially desirable or socially undesirable.

[1] See books by Professor B.F. Skinner: *Walden Two*, 1948, and *Beyond Freedom and Dignity*, 1971.

Hence, to abort anti-social behavior when it is first manifested, by redirection into desirable directions, is the primary
task of the home (where superego control is either learned
or not learned early in life), school, and other social agencies,
such as church, youth organizations, and informal recreational
activities. Where these less abrasive agencies are unable to
divert aggressive anti-social behavior, the police, courts, and
confinement must operate to protect society, or anarchy will
result. No society can tolerate youth as vandals. The doctrine
of *parens patriae* holds that the State has the power through
its courts to act in behalf of the child as a wise parent would.

The juvenile court idea has suffered both in the past and
today from the quality of personnel in its operations. Some
judges, perhaps a third, are not properly qualified to serve:
no college-level training, no legal training or experience, part-
time duty as a judge (perhaps a tradesman by occupation),
no psychological or sociological education. Hasty hearings,
lasting ten to fifteen minutes, are reported.

There had been gross neglect of due process in court proceedings concerning juveniles until the decision entitled *In
Re Gault*[2] in 1967. In that decision, the Supreme Court of
the United States noted that commitment to an institution,
whatever its purposes, amounts to imprisonment, and may
be justified only by a hearing which comports to constitutional
requirements of due process. The Gault case established these
rights: the right to adequate notice of the acts allegedly giving
the court jurisdiction over the child; the right to be rep-
resented by counsel and to have counsel appointed if
indigent; the right to remain silent in face of an accusation
(he need not testify against himself); the right of self and
counsel to confront and cross-examine witnesses against him,
and to supoena witnesses in his defense; the right to a speedy
and public trial conducted in an orderly manner before an
impartial judge; the right of reasonable notice of the charges
and time and place of the trial; and, finally, no child was
to be deprived of *life, liberty, or property* without the
safeguards of due process of law. Additionally, the right to
appellate review is granted. Left undecided in the Gault case

[2] *In Re Gault*, 387 U.S. 1 (1967).

were two crucial trial rights, namely the right to a trial by jury and the right to have one's involvement in illegal activity proved by a high standard of proof. These latter issues are the subject of current litigation, and are discussed later in this chapter.

In the past, and in some areas even today, most juveniles have had the worst of both worlds: they have been charged with many offenses which are not chargeable for adults (for example, truancy) and they have not had due process protection of the laws enjoyed by adults. They have, in fact, been regarded as *non-persons*. Hearsay evidence, absence of counsel, absence of records, hasty decisions on unfounded accusations, parental desire to be rid of the child, non-appeal, and summary disposition to reformatories without careful background work-up of the case, have been all too common, and continue to this day. Private lawyers in juvenile courts were and are typically small-fee practitioners who make their living from minor criminal and civil matters, and the juvenile court generated its own system of complicity which did not encourage the kinds of informal bargaining arrangements that were found in the criminal courts. Among the occupational hazards found to exist for lawyers in the juvenile court were the modest and undependable fees; the lack of significance of informal bargaining and negotiated pleas; lack of fringe benefits; and a possible conflict of interest between a juvenile client and his parents. Where the same lawyer *represents* both parents and child, this conflict of interest must indeed be a grave threat to justice in such cases. The juvenile court is often a low-status court, with role-identity confusion for both judges and lawyers.

It is now quite clear that the requirements of *Miranda v. Arizona*[3] bind the police in dealing with youthful law violators, and several courts haved ruled that a child's statement to police or probation officers without the advice of counsel is inadmissible at the juvenile court hearing, unless his constitutional rights were competently and intelligently waived both by the child and by his parent or guardian. Probation officers, like police, must inform the child and his parents

[3] *Miranda v. Arizona*, 384 U.S. 436 (1966).

of their right to counsel and to remain silent, and, in order to encourage the free flow of information at the intake point, several statutes and the National Council on Crime and Delinquency Model Rules for Juvenile Courts provide that uncounselled statements made at intake may not be used in the court proceeding.

There is wide recognition of the danger of labeling juveniles as delinquents, which may create more delinquency than it solves. The first arrest is to be avoided at almost all cost; official processes must be the last resort and be invoked only where clearly necessary for public safety, and after all possible non-judicial alternatives have been fully investigated and found not to be workable. This is not to recommend a series of probationary dispositions which continue the juvenile in his criminogenic environment, leading usually to increasingly serious deviancy—even to the homicide of a police officer.

Experience and common sense indicate that for all chance offenders probation constitutes the only sensible disposition. The same is true of most first offenders. When wisely granted and when supervision is of high quality, probation serves society's interest best by protecting the individual from the criminal and the criminal stamp most likely to turn him into a habitual criminal and it costs the taxpayers perhaps one tenth as much as imprisonment. Most penologists agree that few steps would be more immediately beneficial in the improvement of the administration of criminal justice than wide-scale extension of probation and raising the quality of probation services.

But for many children and youths in trouble, probation is not the answer. To return to his home and neighborhood an individual of any age who has acquired the habit of delinquency or criminal behavior, who has deep seated maladjustments, or whose delinquent behavior springs from drug abuse, brutality or immorality or the breakdown of satisfactory relationships in the home or from membership in a vicious neighborhood gang, is usually to do a disservice to the individual, to society and to the cause of probation. Where misconduct is habitual, serious, criminal, or symptomatic of deep-rooted causes, probation, as usually supervised by over-worked officers, has little chance of success.

Let us recognize at once, however, that if probation is contra-indicated for many offenders, the only alternative to it available to most courts often does even greater harm to the individual and to society. That alternative is imprisonment in the jail, the state school, reformatory, or prison.

In various states children in trouble may be labeled as abandoned infants, battered, neglected, dependent, sexually abused, retarded, emotionally disturbed, runaways, school dropouts or kick-outs, unwed mothers, drug users, incorrigibles, persons in need of supervision, or delinquents. They may be categorized in many other ways. These archaic labels are too often damaging, may prevent a child from getting the help he needs, or reflect no more than the superficiality of the investigation made by a welfare department, the police, court, school, or some other agency. The labels we use often reflect only the child's age, which agency first discovered the child, and his failed response to a destructive environment.

Our society tends to ignore children in trouble, usually preferring to remove them from sight. Many citizens demand severe punishment. An adult who would punish a child stricken with measles or leukemia would be considered insane; yet youngsters battered or neglected by alcoholic parents, children who run away because their homes are without love, or because they are being laughed at and psychologically hurt at school, or because they are being beaten or raped, are often ignored or punished. Some children indeed need at times the protection of the court. Each day it is estimated some three to ten children are severely beaten, many fatally, by parents or adults having custody of the child.

There is a great need for modern detention facilities for juveniles and children who must be sheltered pending disposition of their cases. Use of adult jails is, of course, condemned. Youths have hanged themselves while confined for minor charges in adult jails; others have been the victims of sexual assaults by adult inmates. The trauma of confinement even overnight is serious for an immature child and should be avoided always where any other disposition is available.

Under juvenile court law, a child may be held in detention before his adjudicatory hearing on several grounds: that he is a potential runaway, that he must be held for pending proceedings in another jurisdiction, and most controversially, that he constitutes a danger to himself or to the community. Thus, juvenile court law recognizes the legitimacy of preventive detention. However, emphasis has been placed on procedural controls over the detention process. Many states have established detention hearing provisions which must be held promptly after admission to detention, usually within twenty-four or forty-eight hours. The problem lies in the non-availability of suitable places for such detention.

In all but a handful of states, a child of sixteen years of age or over who is charged with an act which, if committed by an adult, would constitute a felony, may, after a full investigation and hearing, be transferred from the juvenile court to the criminal court for prosecution as an adult. Under the United States Supreme Court case of *Kent v. United States*,[4] such a transfer must be preceded by a judicial hearing, with counsel, testing the necessity for the transfer; the State must exhaust all possible juvenile correctional alternatives before denying the child the benefits of the juvenile justice system.

A great gap exists between the rhetoric of the juvenile court philosophy and the reality of juvenile court practice. The court must have its resources beefed up, and at the same time the legal protections for the juvenile must be increased and made operative everywhere (which is not the case in many jurisdictions today). Model regional juvenile court programs with related detention and diagnostic facilities are needed to demonstrate the possibilities of a fully implemented juvenile court.

Juvenile delinquency begins at a very early age. By six or eight years of age, a predelinquent child may be the subject of a considerable folder on file at a police station. Obviously, this is the time when intervention is indicated and the full resources of society should be mobilized to deter further

---

[4] *Kent v. United States*, 383 U.S. 541 (1966).

growth in anti-social directions. Society is indeed partially responsible for every delinquent's predicament of being in violation of law. Society continues to spawn misfits such as Lee Harvey Oswald, whose childhood showed every indication of the troubles he later acted out: hostility, violence, incorrigibility, truancy, no friends, no affection for others (including his mother), egocentric gratifications, non-conformity, alienation and withdrawal. This perpetuation of his kind of *loser* is the great defect in today's society; its cost is impossible to overestimate.

Efforts to cushion the behavioral problems of adolescents are not usually received sympathetically by the public. The notion that punishment will cure is deeply instilled. The Old Testament's *eye for an eye,* and *spare the rod and spoil the child,* are mistakenly believed by many to be the answer to the escalating crime statistics. Over one million (1,052,000) juvenile delinquency cases, excluding traffic offenses, were handled by juvenile courts in the United States in 1970. These children represent 2.8 per cent of all children aged ten through seventeen in the country. In 1970, there was again an increase in the number of juvenile court delinquency cases over the previous year. The increase for 1970 was six per cent as compared to an increase in the child population aged ten through seventeen of only two per cent. Delinquency remains primarily a boys' problem, but the disparity between the number of boys' and girls' delinquency court cases is narrowing. For many years, boys were referred to court for delinquency about four times as often as girls. Because of the recent faster increase in girls' cases as compared to boys', the ratio was reduced to about three to one by 1970. (The preceding statistics are quoted from *Juvenile Court Statistics, 1970,* compiled by the U.S. Department of Health, Education, and Welfare.)

The juvenile law area of legal practice is in turmoil today as consequence of recent court decisions and news media exposure[5] of the malpractices of many *courts.* There is little money for lawyers in such practice, except for cases involving rich clients. Any act, which if he were an adult would be

---

[5] Series in *The Christian Science Monitor,* 1971.

a crime (other than a traffic offense), may be charged to a juvenile. An obscene phone call allegedly make by a fifteen year old boy named Gault[6] resulted in his commitment to a state training school which was to extend to his twenty-first birthday unless changed by judicial act. This sentence was overruled by the Supreme Court of the United States, with far-reaching effects for all juvenile courts. Young Gault's constitutional rights had been completely disregarded by the lower court in his case.

Juvenile courts have legitimate roles in adjudicating domestic relations cases of neglect, dependency, adoption, and delinquency. These courts have authority to commit youths to training schools for the duration of their minority. Unfortunately, some parents and/or guardians of juveniles have consented to commitment of their wards to State training schools in the mistaken idea that such a step was in the best interests of a *difficult* child. Commitment is clearly to be the last resort for all but the most refractive cases. There is a great need for half-way houses which will shelter youths who are not yet hard core delinquents and/or need a transition period between confinement and full release to open society.

The probation officer is a key official in the juvenile court operation. His case-load must be reasonable and his professional competence beyond question. While *informal adjustment* through the provision of probation-type services without a court adjudication is still encouraged, a number of states have provided that such activity be limited to a two or three month period, and have also insisted that a child who maintains his innocence has the right to a court hearing and need not accept the benevolent but sometimes irritating offers of assistance from probation officers.

Police contacts with the juvenile can have a far-reaching effect on the future roads he may choose to travel. While the Juvenile Court is always hailed as the most significant of the agencies that deal with delinquents, the police have contacts with many more misbehaving and outright delinquent children than does the juvenile court. About one-half of all children picked up or arrested by the police are referred

[6] *In Re* Gault, 387 U.S. 1 (1967).

to the juvenile court. The other half are handled independently by the police. Moreover, the police make the decisions as to which ones they will handle and how. In addition to dealing with delinquents, police have many informal encounters with children on the streets and in places where children loiter. Here they exercise general supervision as part of their function of maintaining order and protecting younger children from harm. The police exercise an extraordinary degree of authority quite independently of the juvenile court. Especially among young and minor delinquents, the police department is the one official agency that the child sees. It is extremely important that police understand and exercise well this vast power that they have.

It is going to take a gigantic effort on the part of all—the family, the schools, the churches, the community organizations, the police, and the juvenile justice system—if we are going to curb the ever-swelling tide of the *youthful offender*.

Drugs have created a whole new ball game in juvenile court operations and functions. Today's youth involved in drug abuse is a new type of respondent and a new disposition is required on the part of the court. Decisions relative to disposition of such cases are extremely complicated; where hard drugs are in question, the chance of rehabilitation is almost zero. Drugs have made a new profile of the juvenile offender. Theft and burglary are numbers one and two in frequency, but drugs, number three, are related to the first two. For female delinquents, involvement with drug abuse is almost one hundred percent.

The following quotation from Kenney and Pursuit[7] summarizes the juvenile court situation today:

> In recognition of the immaturity and the potential of young people, a philosophy has developed which, for the most part, labels the anti-social acts of children as behavior problems rather than as criminal behavior. But despite the fact that the machinery for dealing with juvenile delinquency is basically protective in nature and aimed at rehabilitation, the fact remains that it is sometimes neces-

[7] Kenney, John P., and Pursuit, Dan G.: *Police Work With Juveniles.* Springfield, Thomas, 1965, p. 43.

sary to deprive children of their liberty and parents of the companionship of their children at home. Because these are important rights,
many of the safeguards afforded the adult person charged with crime
must be observed for the protection of the child, of his family, and
of the community. The machinery for deciding when these rights
shall be abrogated is centered largely in the juvenile court, or where
separate juvenile courts do not exist as such, in their counterparts.

As we noted earlier, the Gault case left undecided the issue
of the right to trial by jury. A recent decision handed down
by the Supreme Court in *McKeiver et al v. Pennsylvania* rejects the contention that juveniles have the right to jury trials.
Judge Orman W. Ketcham, Superior Court of the District
of Columbia, in an article in *Criminal Justice Newsletter*
of November 29, 1971, stated:

> . . . it seems probable that the Supreme Court has called a halt
> to the extension of adult due process requirements to juvenile trials.
> The Court held that a right to trial by jury is not an 'essential of
> due process and fair treatment' required to insure fundamental fair-
> ness in juvenile proceedings. In so doing the Court rejected Justice
> Black's view that the due process clause of the 14th Amendment
> requires the application of *all* the Bill of Rights to state juvenile
> procedural systems. This decision may well mark the Court's final
> chapter on the adjudicative phase of juvenile justice.

Justice Blackmun, speaking for the Chief Justice and
Justices Stewart and White, wrote the prevailing opinion in
the case of *McKeiver et al v. Pennsylvania*. The reasons for
the decision as quoted in Judge Ketcham's article were:

> 1. A jury's verdict on the facts is not an essential element in
> a fair trial.
> 2. A state has the right to experiment with juvenile procedures
> without the encumbrance of juries.
> 3. Trial by jury would not cure the existing defects in the juvenile
> justice system.
> 4. To grant the right to a jury trial would 'remake the juvenile
> proceeding into a fully adversary process' inimical to the informal
> juvenile court ideal.
> 5. To require adjudicative procedures identical with adult crimi-
> nal proceedings would deprive the juvenile court of its reason for
> a separate existence.

Justice Blackmun stated that what is needed is neither criminal
nor civil procedure, but a balance between procedural orderli-

ness and preservation of the good motives, special concern and paternal attention of the juvenile court tradition.

Justice White, in his concurring opinion in the *McKeiver* case, indicated that since he sees the juvenile justice system as *eschewing blameworthiness and punishment for evil choice,* the jury as a curb on judicial power is not needed in juvenile proceedings.

As Judge Ketcham stated, the suspicion exists that the practical consequences in the administrative functioning of state juvenile courts played a large part in the Court's decision to deny juveniles a right to a jury trial.

It appears that for the time being the juvenile courts will continue to serve as the public repository of the private sector's failures—a system of kibbutzim to which the price of entry is a purse-snatching. A specialized court, sensitive to modern psychological and sociological concepts can do a great deal of good for *children with a problem.* To view children in trouble as *problem children* is clearly untenable and contra-indicated.

To reintegrate youthful offenders back into noncriminal adjustments, the help of non-professionals such as volunteers, and others, is needed. The run-away statistics of juvenile anti-social conduct are shocking warnings of the social dyscontrol now existing and which must somehow be aborted. Diversion of youthful offenders who are guilty of *juvenile status offenses* i.e., charges which can only be brought against persons of juvenile age such as truancy, ungovernable, or running away from home, should be made to a private agency.

CHAPTER VII

DRUG ABUSE

IN THIS BRIEF condensation of a many faceted problem, the news reporter's five W's will be used: who, what, where, when, and why.

Who: One in five students, ages thirteen to seventeen, is a *relatively frequent drug user,* according to Dr. Matthew P. Dumont, formerly of the National Institute of Mental Health.[1] Forty-five percent of New York City high school, tenth through twelfth grade students, are more than occasional users of some *psychoactive* drug, as of the fall semester of 1972, according to the Fleishmann Commission.[2] There is little doubt that the extent of drug abuse is much greater than reported or than many think. Parents and teachers are deceived; police cannot identify and charge many users; and society seems almost helpless to cope with the problem. Adults show an unbelievable incidence of drug abuse. Tranquilizers are taken daily by millions of people, in addition to diet pills and pep pills. We are indeed a nation of drug users. Apparently the idea has taken hold that there is a pill to solve every problem of life; ingestion of drugs without medical supervision is commonplace, and there is easy availability of drugs to all levels of society.

What: All medicines and drugs are toxic when ingested in quantities not medically prescribed. Alcohol is by far the greatest abuse problem, with some six million alcoholics and countless so-called social drinkers in this country. The costs of alcoholism are astronomical in terms of industrial accidents, motor vehicle accidents (over half of all fatal motor vehicle accidents involve alcohol), loss of work days, and health

[1] *Christian Science Monitor,* Sept. 18, 1971, p. 7.
[2] *New York Times News Service,* Oct. 13, 1972.

deterioration related to chronic illness and early death.

Other drugs abused are the narcotics (cocaine, heroin, morphine, and marijuana); the tranquilizing barbiturates (Nembutal,® Seconal,® Tuinal,® and Amytal®); and the stimulating amphetamines (Benzedrine,® Dexedrine®); together with combinations of these and other mood-altering hallucinogenics and psychoactives, such as mescaline, LSD-25, aerosols and model airplane glue. All of these have the potential for causing addiction and/or psychic or emotional dependence. Their use, except under medical supervision, is dangerous and illegal. Their prescription by a physician for therapy is, of course, medically approved for depression, overweight, narcolepsy, Parkinsonism, insomnia, and as an anesthesia for pain.

Where: Drug abuse occurs at all levels of the social scale, at all ages (even neonates are born addicted), and throughout the world. Certain countries which are the chief suppliers or processers of illegal drugs are finding that many of their own young people are drug abusers; this is helping to bring pressure on authorities in these countries to prohibit all drug production (particularly the opium poppy). Southeast Asia, Asia Minor (Turkey) and Latin-America are well-known centers for drug traffic. The United States Government is now subsidizing farmers who formerly grew opium poppies in Turkey in order to eradicate, as far as possible, the production source; whether this will prove of value remains to be seen; other sources will become available.

Apparently, ghetto areas for large cities are most involved in drug abuse, but its spread to affluent suburban areas is now a fact, creating problems for many middle and upper-class families.

When: The epidemiology of drug abuse has shown a dramatic rise in rates since 1960. The Viet-Nam War has created a special problem, with hard-drug addiction estimated to number at least 100,000 among returned veterans. This may be the most costly fall-out of that war. There has been a rise in drug addiction following every war, including the Civil War of 1861–65. It was, ironically, the treatment of morphine addicts among Civil War veterans that led to widespread use of heroin. In 1898, it was discovered that this new *wonder drug* was able to keep a morphine addict from suffering withdrawal symptoms and was thought to be non-addicting itself. It was four or five years later before it was learned that heroin was four times stronger than morphine and at least twice as addicting. Today, ninety percent of the narcotic addicts are on heroin.

All authorities agree that recent figures of drug abuse show alarming increases in both relative and actual incidences of drug abuse in this country and world-wide. The *youth culture* apparently has embraced drug abuse as its trademark.

Rehabilitation (abstinence) from abuse of hard drugs is estimated to be about fifty per cent among those who stay in a clinic's program; for those who attempt to kick the habit on their own, the rate is thought to be two to eight per cent success over a three-year period. The rate of cure may be only one per cent.

Why: Multiple reasons, many specious and irrational, have been advanced relative to why drug abuse occurs. A simple explanation would appear to be this: people take drugs because they get something from it. A chemical cocoon is sought to envelope the abuser and to shield him from the real world from which he flees; the real world is too threatening, too painful, and he cannot cope with it. Drugs enable him to *cop-out.* Some few individuals become addicted after medically-prescribed use, but most addicts admit they graduate from alcohol or mild drugs to hard drugs (some eighty percent of addicts begin with marijuana).

The grave likelihood of permanent addiction evidently does not deter experimentation with drugs. That a pill or bottle can become master of one's life is not realized by many addicts until they are *hooked.* Less than one per cent of hard-core addicts are estimated to be ever rehabilitated—a dismal prognosis indeed, and in itself sufficient reason to dissuade any *experimentation.* As with alcoholics, each day is a test whether drugs will win out; *recovering alcoholics* is the term used by Alcoholics Anonymous—it would apply certainly to drug addicts, who really are never *cured* until dead.

Most authorities agree that addiction is related to per-

sonality: some individuals from a combination of constitutional factors and social conditioning from life experiences
seem particularly prone to psychic dependence; the craving
for drugs is initially psychological, not in response to physical
needs. The problem initially is from the neck up, not the
neck down. Sedation or stimulation, with euphoria or a feeling
of well-being, and escape from reality is the effect from drugs.
Obviously, efficient functioning in today's competitive and
aggressive society is impossible for drug addicts. Most
drug abusers are diagnosed as of marginal personality integration; drug abuse is a symptom of their mental or emotional illness. They have one common characteristic: they
feel they cannot function even on a low level of performance
without the crutch which drugs provide for them. Drugs are
often abused in a social setting with others who are seriously
maladjusted and in rebellion against the square world. This
aspect of drug abuse and the counterculture nature of the drug
abuse set adds a serious complication for many youths.

Some addicts apparently have adjusted to their habit and
function with relative success while continuing a controlled
form of abuse, working and masking their addiction at the
same time. Employers are attempting to identify these persons
through medical screenings, and Labor Unions are trying to
fight this problem, since *high* employees may be dangerous
around machinery.

Juvenile drug users are especially vulnerable to peer
influence; many will experiment with drugs in order not to
be *chicken*, and in order to *belong to the crowd*. The turbulence of adolescence, requiring many adjustments of both
psychological and physiological nature, has been fully
covered in previous chapters. The *thrill* aspects of drugs,
their forbidden nature, and the mistaken idea of many adolescents that they can take or leave drugs, are factors to be considered. That a felony conviction for drug abuse can be a life-
long handicap is apparently disregarded by many youths.

Fatal consequences of experimentation with heroin, glue,
aerosols or other solvents, LSD, and other *bad trips* seem
to be of little or no deterrence to others. An abuse-prone
individual will often continue on from mild to severe drugs

until he is a confirmed drug user and the road back is virtually blocked.

Contrary to popular belief, few adolescents are introduced to drugs by big-time *pushers*—peers do it. The myth that the pusher is usually a long-haired bum has no basis in fact—a peer group member who sells to maintain his own habit is by far more common.

In contrast, the adult abuser of drugs commonly has a history of personal and social maladjustment. He is a *loser* in life's race, and the chemical curtain which alcohol and drugs provide is too rewarding for him to reject.

The ghetto with its segregation and deprivation is a natural habitat for drug abuse. When the pressure is too great from environmental and/or emotional stresses, the drug abuser will retreat to the detachment from reality which drugs provide, no matter what the cost or the resulting eventual aggravation of his problems. The fractured and fragile family patterns often seen in the ghetto are both the result and cause of the instability of that world of the street. However, addiction is in no sense restricted to *over the tracks*.

The cost in dollars to maintain an addict is estimated to be from $75 to $150 per day. Few people can legitimately earn that much money, and crime would be perhaps half eliminated if addiction were removed. Robbery, shoplifting, burglary, forgery, assault, and prostitution are the usual crimes associated with drug abuse. The inner city is the target area for drug traffic control; the underground of the criminal world is its medium for operations. The millions of dollars changing hands daily in organized crime operations is the life-blood of drug traffic. Its eradication will be most difficult. A mobilization today of the nation's public health, social and educational agencies is imperative.

Two additional potentially quite dangerous side effects from LSD-25 are: (1) the broken chromosome chain, with future generations subject to possible genetic defects, and (2) the *flash-back*, which is a psychotic episode which may occur as late as two years after the last use, when stress may reintroduce the LSD-25 *trips*. Organic brain damage may be initiated on the first *trip*. One ounce of LSD can provide 300,000 doses.

A final word relative to marijuana: this drug is not believed to be addictive, yet it produces a form of intoxication that can result in unpredictable and occasionally violent behavior. It is legally classified with the narcotics for the purpose of control; chemically it is different from the *hard narcotics*. In about one-third of the states, the laws do not distinguish between marijuana and the harder drugs, such as heroin and cocaine. Penalties are harsh for possession (perhaps two to five years) and for sale (five or more years). First offenders for possession or use are often treated more leniently. Today there is a two-year minimum penalty for federal marijuana violators—the same as for heroin violators. New bills in the Congress would allow judges to use their discretion; and no jail sentences would be required. They would also allow first time offenders to have their convictions eventually erased from their court records. These less drastic penalties are being recommended by legal, prison, and health authorities.

New classifications of each drug are needed, depending on its (1) potential for abuse; (2) acceptance for medical use; and (3) the degree of dependence (psychological as well as physiological) it causes.

Controversy surrounds the *no-knock* provision laws which would allow police to enter a house on a specific court warrant without first knocking, to prevent disposal of the evidence. At this writing, the provisions of the law, in the opinion of many police officers, make it difficult to obtain convictions for possession of narcotics, when pushers have an opportunity to destroy evidence prior to the search.

As William H. Stringer pointed out in an article in the *Christian Science Monitor* on February 11, 1971, "Beyond any evidence of possible physical impairment, a major peril from pot smoking is its stealthy engendering of apathy, altered life goals, and false concepts of reality, among frequent users."

While it is true that many of the youngsters who experiment with marijuana will go no further than the experimentation stage and may come to no serious harm as a result, a significant number will. The so-called *soft drug* users, once they are introduced to the drug subculture, find it all too easy to continue on to hard drugs. The problems or attitudes which brought them to the experimentation with marijuana in the first place are not solved or changed by its use—indeed, may be amplified. And, unfortunately, rarely will an adolescent admit or acknowledge that there is any likelihood of his getting hurt or that there is any danger involved in his trying the various drugs. Thus, treatment or the halting of participation in the abuse of drugs in most cases presents a great many obstacles. Until and unless the adolescent is motivated in a direction away from drugs, the path downward is steep and sure.

Since the general topic of drug abuse first merited inclusion in a text dealing with the psychology of the youthful offender—approximately in 1968—the attention which now must be given to it has taken a quantum jump. Let no reader be deceived as to the deadly serious effects of drug abuse as it threatens the very core of our social order today. We are in deep trouble.

In 1967, one of our nation's largest cities had fifty-eight juvenile narcotic cases reported in a twelve-month's period. In September of 1970 there were fifty-eight such cases reported in the same city for a thirty-day period. Since cases reported to the police have little true relation to actual numbers of cases—perhaps one in ten—the sheer numbers of narcotic cases are shocking. Today, three years later, true figures are believed to have been multiplied in geometric ratio.

During late 1972, a House Select Committee on Crime in Los Angeles heard testimony from high school pupils in that area which alleged that as many as seventy-five percent of all high school pupils were using drugs, and were getting high every day. Drug abuse was said to begin at the fifth grade.

If Americans are becoming increasingly drug dependent, is there any relationship to the one billion dollar plus being spent every year to advertise over-the-counter and prescription drugs? Four of the five top network TV spenders are drug companies, according to testimony before the National Council of Charities in November, 1972. Drug use is two to four times greater (two billion prescriptions each year) than in some other countries which seem to have the same general level of health. Perhaps it is no coincidence that drug abuse is now *rampant* in its first TV-raised generation. *Pill-popping* for every minor discomfort is now routine for the entire family in many homes; obesity, depression, grief, frustrations, sleeplessness, and *nerves* are considered to be especially valid justifications for the belief that there is a *chemical for everything.*

Clearly, a reorientation of the values of our social order is imperatively needed: a philosophy of life which is rooted in humanistic values, of work ethic, of morality, and of respect for health and life. Unless this can be achieved, the continued existence of society as we know it is in jeopardy.

The following account of a school drug-abuse program was contributed by one of the author's students:

For approximately two years, this student was assigned to a program on juvenile drug abuse. This assignment was outside the enforcement field. My time was spent in schools, from elementary to colleges, rapping with students about drugs. After spending time with students, it was apparent that parents should be included in the program. This was done on a segregated basis. Students and parents were not contacted together.

The following format was used: This officer would go into a school. A period of the school day was allotted, and students were contacted in small groups. Large assemblies were a waste of time. I usually had six hours of classes per day, and stayed from three to five days at each school. After this program was finished, a night meeting was held at the school with parents, businessmen and teachers.

After reading the chapter on drug abuse, I would agree with the statements it contained. The only faults found in the chapter were faults of omission and not content.

In the field of drugs, it was found that inhalents were a commonly used drug in elementary and junior high schools. The most popular was airplane glue (which was mentioned) but as glue became more difficult for pre-teenagers and young teens to acquire, other inhalents were substituted. Most popular are: paint-thinner, gasoline, and hairspray. All of these inhalents are easy to obtain and are extremely dangerous to users. In high schools, marijuana and pills were most popular, but inhalents were still in great demand.

The reason given by students for using drugs sounded like a recording. The main reasons stated were: my friends use drugs and they talked me into trying them; my parents get high on booze, why can't I use drugs; they make me feel good; and, perhaps the saddest reason of all: the use of drugs to get even with parents.

It did not seem to matter what part of town the program was

given, affluent, middle class or poor, black or white, the same drugs were popular and the main reasons for using them stayed consistent.

The main pushers of drugs in these schools were other students and this was true in every school visited. This was very difficult to get over to adults; they insisted that this was not possible.

In fact, parents were much more difficult to deal with than students. The adults admitted that a problem existed, but were reluctant to believe that their child could be involved. After the group meetings were over, many of these adults would come up and tell of neighbor children, friends of their child, and children of relatives who they suspected of using drugs. Very seldom would they speak of a drug problem of their own child.

The reaction parents showed when informed of drug abuse by their own child was interesting. A mother we contacted and informed of her fifteen year old's arrest for drug abuse had the following reaction: What am *I* going to do? What will *my* friends think? *I* will not be able to look anyone in the eye. Not once did any concern for the child show.

Although this was an extreme reaction, many others were encountered along these lines. The first concern of many parents was their social standing and the stigma of having a child who was a drug user; their second concern was the child. One might think if this order of concern was reversed, the possibility of helping the child would be greatly enhanced.

In closing, I must state that being close to the problem did not show how to solve it. It seems everyone is in the same boat. It is impossible to read the papers or correspond with other agencies without hearing of new drug programs. Federal, state, and local agencies all have programs. Groups of private citizens, civic clubs, and churches also have programs and the problem continues to grow. More groups and programs do not appear to be the answer, as they all go their separate ways, and at times jealously conceal facts from each other. Some claim fantastic results in rehabilitation, which leaves one to wonder where they gather their statistics.

If all these efforts could be concentrated and worked together instead of separately, some inroads into the problem of juvenile drug abuse may be obtained. The direction we are now committed to is a losing proposition.

New York State's Governor Rockefeller early in 1973 recommended that legislation be enacted in his state which would mandate severe penal sentences—up to life—for convicted pushers and abusers of hard drugs (e.g., heroin), to preclude plea bargaining, suspended sentence, probation, or parole. He stated that New York State had recently spent one billion dollars in a futile effort to control addiction and that stern measures were imperative. Such legislation would present grave difficulties to the courts; long trials would undoubtedly be required.

CHAPTER VIII

PUNISHMENT AS
SOCIAL OBJECTIVE

THE QUOTATION: "Punishment as therapy is semantic acrobatics," is an excellent master sentence for this unit of the psychology of the youthful offender. The Old Testament idea of dire vengeance for wrong doing, of an eye for an eye, or *spare the rod, spoil the child*, is today believed to be not only antedated but even viciously harmful in its counter-productive aspects. The purpose of correctional action is to correct; it is not to make the offender less adjusted and more sick. To *hate the sin, not the sinner*, must be the goal of judges, parents, police, teachers, and social workers.

To punish is to harm; it is not in any sense curative or restorative; it is upside-down thinking. Punishment does have a partially effective immediate deterrence value; at the moment—for that instance of behavior—it is of some value as a control. It does not, however, get at the root cause or causes of misbehavior. It does not change the root causes; in fact, it may make these basic causes more potent as negative harmful shapers of behavior. For example, the felon who has *paid his debt* by prison time may feel he is now at liberty to commit more crime.

The child who is whipped feels he has been absolved of his responsibility for that misbehavior. He may not have internalized any learnings from the punishment other than that he hates the punisher and that he will be more careful not to be caught in the future.

This is not to advocate a regime for any child free of controls. Children must be trained to accept and expect the consequences for their actions. A child not out of bed in time for school will be tardy. This usually puts him in an uncomfortable position. The rationale for family rules can be explained to young children (ages four to eight) and by use of operant conditioning with reinforcement only for desired behavior and all physical punishment abandoned, children can be inducted, with help of great patience and forebearance by elders, into responsible social roles at home, school, and society. The underlying causes of his antisocial behavior may well be some degree of psychopathology, distorted reality from childhood exposure to criminogenic factors, inability to succeed at school or to earn a living (no trade, illiteracy, low mental and emotional maturity), physical and/or mental defects which are rarely if ever diagnosed, and with remedial measures neglected or absent.

Conformity and compliance based on fear only is worth nothing. A police department whose members obey regulations only when superiors are present has no real discipline. Control which is not self-control and self-motivated is a sham. No supervision can be always present. Hence, the goal must be to instill the abstractions of duty, honor, dedication and moral suasion, not the specific corrections of punishments, sanctions, and psychological or physical trauma.

The results over the centuries of the indiscriminate use of punishment have been dismal. Man has not become better as consequence of the most barbarous and inhumane punishments. He continues to show his animal-like, vicious nature. In fact, he is only *papered-over* with civilization. Physical blows, confinement, psychological blows (derision, scorn, invidious comparisons, vicious demeaning critism) are severe and counter-productive. They decrease the self-control potential of the involved person, lessen his self-confidence, damage his self-image, and confirm his lessened status in his peer group. *What others think of me, I will think of me, and what I think of me, I am.*

This is not to say that some psychopathic individuals must not at times be confined (*sick* persons who are mentally ill, depraved, degenerate, and defective). Some must be permanently removed from open society for their welfare and that of others, when their capacity for self-control is inadequate. A role remains for constructive criticism and psychological controls—children should be guided by operant Skinnerian conditioning, to shape behavior in socially desired directions. The egocentric and selfish hedonism we all show at times must be guided by rewards, non-rewards, and in some instances, by rational punishment (for example, a fine for a moving traffic violation). However, the kids who misbehave the most are invariably the kids who have been beaten the most. The other extreme, where no effective control has been used and internalized, is equally to be deplored, and results in seriously maladjusted individuals who are consequently unfit to cope with life's problems.

In all punishment there is the involvement of the punisher, usually in an emotionally angry setting where he has *lost his cool.* When we are not calm and collected, we think emotionally, with the so-called *old brain;* the *new brain,* the reasoning area of the frontal areas of the brain, is *short-circuited.* This accounts for the unreasonable, irrational acts we perform under emotional stress and which we look back upon by saying, "I must not have been myself." In these instances, children are maimed and killed (more children are killed by their parents than die from childhood diseases), and many violent acts of homicide and assault result. Some so-called police brutality undoubtedly is related to loss of *cool* in provoking situations (some excessive use of force does occasionally occur in police work, but such behavior is punishable and is decried by police commanders). Brutality against the police is common; one in every ten police officers is assaulted each year. This gets little or no publicity by news media.

The punisher cannot wear two hats equally well. The parent who buys his son a new bicycle is also the one who must at times take away its use when necessary. The punisher in his role leaves emotional scars which cannot be erased. This predicament teaches that punishment which is in retribution, to get even, or to ventilate displaced aggression (for example, the father loses his job, beats his son that evening for a minor infraction), is dangerous and *always* counter-productive. *The punishment does not correct the root cause for which punishment seems to be in order at that time.* The punisher gets some emotional relief by his displaced aggression and the physical act of administering the paddling does ventilate his frustration, but at a high cost to both himself and the weaker subordinate second party. Children do resent greatly the use of superior physical power by adults to force compliance. Parents who use corporal punishment beyond the early few (perhaps age three to five) years of life were usually, themselves, subjected to excessive corporal punishment during childhood. We do not need successive generations reflecting themselves like mirrors locked face-to-face down an endless corridor of despair. All acts generate reactions. Does the beating really shape the child to long-range behavior goals? Could these goals not have been reached better by psychological rather than physical controls? The therapeutic approach is that of the clinician M.D.—not to blame—just try to effect a *cure*. The *cure* is the sought-for goal of self control and emotional equilibrium.

Compliance based on law, regulations, or rules is not the answer to control of human behavior. Self-control, self-discipline, the Communistic ideal of the *withering away of the state* (which has *not* occurred in China or the U.S.S.R.), where police, army, jails, will no longer be needed, is a dream which man's basically selfish nature apparently will not yet permit. In Freudian Theory, man's animal nature and selfish egocentrisms make Utopian schemes of society unrealistic to expect.

Perhaps the theory of Dr. B.F. Skinner will in time prevail even in the U.S.A.: man will be rewarded (reinforced) for desired behavior and non-rewarded, even punished severely, for deviant behavior. This will be Orwell's *World of 1984*, with computerized information on file for each of us, a minimum of personal freedom, closed circuit input for all news, unapproved ideas not to be circulated, man's very existence subject to minute controls, and society regimented as is notably the case in Red China today. To be sure, V.D. may be eliminated, a minimum of low-quality health services may be readily available (from so-called *barefoot doctors*) there will be no unemployment, and slums will largely disappear, *but at a cost.* The cost is the loss of individual freedom; the collective state absorbs the individual with loss of his identity.

All actions beget reactions; hurts inflicted in immature juveniles are especially to be avoided for they jeopardize the entire life projections of the youth. Emotional *scar tissue* from official sanctions (e.g., *The First Arrest*) prejudice later adjustments, and handicap individuals who have no legitimate cause for such life-long social stigma to be held against them. Juvenile records should be for confidential police use only and expunged at age twenty-one, as many states now require.

The central problem in this discussion of punishment as a social phenomenon is that of the philosophy of life held by both the punisher and the punished (a philosophy of life is a set of values, a frame of reference, a pattern of solutions which are internalized and which guide behavior). If one believes that *Gung-Ho,* bulldozer tactics pay off, then direct physical action will likely be resorted to in problem solving. If more indirect, gentle, and dispassionate behavior has been rewarded by greater success, this pattern will dominate. In police, corrections, or social work there is little doubt that the latter course is to be preferred.

The day when confrontation and adversary-type encounters paid off has long passed. Today's public will no longer tolerate uncouth or aggressive behavior patterns by public servants, and such behavior can only be counter-productive. We need to use the medical model—to cure, not to make more sick. Respect and security are key words to describe optimum interpersonal relations. Corporal punishment of youths and adults has no place in this picture.

We have surely progressed from cave-man days and we must hope that man can some day truly be *homo sapiens*—the thinking man who can reason. This day of enlightened interpersonal relations, of man's humanity to man, will only be achieved when current ideas of the value of *punishment* are no longer believed.

Unfortunately, the above views are not held by some judges, police, corrections, and welfare personnel. So called *hard-*

nose views are difficult to change. Perhaps the key idea of this book is this: that men of good will in positions of authority and decision-making, must interact with humanity and compassion in adversary confrontations such as arrest situations, counseling sessions, and case-work visitations. *There are children with problems, not problem children,* has long been wisely observed. Our aim must be to treat the sick behavior, not aggravate the condition. We must proceed from where the respondent (if a minor) or the accused (if of majority age) now is, with all thought of recriminations, stigma, and retribution put entirely out of mind. Judges should consider the cases of convicted persons not only on the basis of *what* was done, but with regard for *who* the defendant is. This will result in many convicted persons not going to jail at all, who would otherwise be jailed for that offense; at the same time, some persons not incarcerated, or incarcerated for brief periods, would be held much longer, perhaps for decades or life, in confinement because of their chronic psychopathic condition or defective life style, which has not yet responded to treatment.

There is a definite groundswell of public opinion in the direction of much less incarceration for long terms and in favor of local handling of anti-social and criminal acts through half-way houses, heavy use of probation, and all out community efforts to reintegrate offenders into a rehabilitated status. Denmark is a notable example today where long imprisonment has been almost completely abandoned.

The prison is the poorest environment we could devise for treating sick minds and disorganized personalities; prisons are dealing with a clientele (inmates) who have largely already had a life-time of failure. The *reconditioning* of such persons by overworked staffs and in the vicious criminogenic surroundings inevitably indigenous in confinement institutions indeed presents a tremendous challenge, and represents an almost impossible task. Recidivism rates of seventy percent are not surprising, given the task and means to deal with the goal of rehabilitation for the two and one-half millions who pass through our prisons each year, and of the one and one-quarter millions who are continuously confined.

The issue of capital punishment (execution) is today (1973)

much in the public's eye. How can society take a life which may be later redeemed, and be of even great value? (The Nathan Leopold case is a notable example of a successful rehabilitation of a murderer.) But the fact of deterrence may do some good, for if the hangman's noose dangles before one, it *may* cause second thoughts for some; for most murderers it is of no deterrence value. Capital punishment has been declared to be a violation of the provisions in the Constitution of the State of California against cruel and unusual punishment (1972). However, seven states which at one time dropped the death penalty have reinstituted it as a deterrent.

The case of Carole Fugate, convicted at age fifteen of murder as the accomplice of Charles Starkweather in 1958, with half her life already spent behind bars, is apparently an example of the non-use of capital punishment (her tender age was a factor) which today (1973) has a favorable prognosis for both her and society. She appeared on telecasts in 1972 with every indication of a successful rehabilitation. Her release on parole is under study (early 1973). Her future life could be valuable for society; all human life is indeed precious. Innocent people have been executed in the past.

Abolishment of capital punishment would call for an adequate deterrent system to take its place, a system that would guarantee the protection of the innocent. What such system has yet been proposed or proven?

G.B. Shaw once said: "To punish a man you must injure him; to reform a man you must improve him, and men are not improved by injuries."

CHAPTER IX

MENTAL ILLNESS AND YOUTH CRIME

IN CONSIDERING MENTAL illness in adolescents, we should first differentiate between those few who are manifestly full-blown psychotic, living in a dream world, from those who although perhaps severely neurotic, yet are in touch with reality and have insight into their personality maladjustment which is less than wholesome. This is a fine line of distinction, but the criterion to differentiate between these two categories is that a neurotic individual retains insight into his condition, whereas the psychotic individual has lost this insight and is functioning in a cloudy, unreal world, to which he retreats when threatened by stress related to emotional or organic causal factors.

Persons who have lost contact with reality either temporarily or for longer periods of time must be regarded as severely mentally ill and in need of hospital treatment. Such individuals are indeed sick and closed-ward inpatient treatment (institutional care) is indicated for them until they have recovered sufficiently to care for themselves in a protected environment, which, hopefully, will be followed by full restoration to mental health. Although such individuals may be found in public school situations and on our streets, they are, in fact, beyond the capabilities of the preventive and treatment facilities and procedures which are usually available to police, corrections, and social rehabilitation. Accordingly, in this presentation, we will concentrate rather on the child who exhibits abnormal behavior, but still is in touch with reality in more or less some degree.

79

Children respond to environmental shaping, to love and security or the neglect or violence which they may experience. We know that more children die from the battered child syndrome than die from the total of children's diseases. It is estimated that five to eight children are killed every day in this country by parental and custodial abuse. Those who survive are indelibly marked, psychologically as well as physically, and these emotional scars may be grave handicaps for many children as they seek personality integration through the adolescent years.

Lack of cohesiveness of the family means that the family is a fighting society rather than a supportive society—the child must actually strike out even to get some bread with peanut butter on it. When a child is brought up in this kind of environment, he will find, long before he is six years old, that he can solve his problems by striking out, by taking what he will not get otherwise. He finds that this pays off for him; by operant conditioning, it is reinforced. He has satisfaction when he fights, strikes out and hurts people. Since he has never received love, affection and security, he cannot experience these feelings; therefore he grows up cold, dispassionate and vicious. Unquestionably the psychopathology of early childhood begins in such distorted environment. The first eighteen to thirty-six months of life are critical in this shaping.

When children are thwarted, they respond routinely by striking out. We can expect a certain amount of unreasonable acting-out behavior. When this becomes vicious and a pattern, obviously it shows marked abnormality. Much of this overt behavior, as expounded in Freudian psychoanalytic theory, is the result of unconscious motivation. The child is striking out in overt behavior for reasons which he does not understand. An example would be the child who steals something, then as soon as he gets outside the store throws it into the garbage can. Another example would be the child who runs away from home for reasons that he cannot explain, but which clearly are the result of overwhelming stress, of the predisposing experiences and psychological trauma which the child has had, which lead him to respond by anti-social and sometimes even criminal behavior.

The fact of unconscious motivation cannot be denied. We are each of us at any time the result of the shaping psychological and hereditary forces which have brought us, with social conditioning, to what we now are. These shaping forces begin very early in life, in the first weeks and months, and we never forget them. They are indelibly recorded in our nervous systems. This is proven by the facility with which they may be recalled under hypnosis, by open brain surgery, by dream analysis, and by free reverie. We actually record in three dimensions and in color everything that happens to us, even long before we have words to express it.

A certain amount of hostility is natural for children. Children of tender ages do not use words to express their hostility; they strike. However, the child soon begins to use words. This built-in hostility is one of the key ideas of Freudian theory. Egocentricity, the *id,* this seething cauldron of our emotions, is part of our primitive ancestral inheritance. Actually, we are covered by a thin veneer of civilization—a little bit of drugs, a little bit of alcohol, a little fear, a little fever, and the individual becomes a vicious animal. He is not concerned with anyone but himself, as is shown in mass panic catastrophies where crowds trample others to death seeking to escape from fires, sinkings of ships, and in war hysteria.

Perhaps to expect man to live in a civilized way, considering the short 15,000 years or so we have been even partly civilized (in terms of the 1,750,000 years or longer that man has existed in relatively his present form) is to expect the impossible. The consequence is that the children will show hostility. We must expect them to show it. In fact, the child who shows no hostility is a sick child. But when a child seizes upon hostility as his *modus operandi* for solution of most of his problems, obviously he is crossing over a line of demarcation and demonstrating a need for therapy.

The school situation is one which we must closely scrutinize, because there we often judge children in terms of adult standards. We expect all children to perform equally—but nature and nurture did not make them equal. They were not made equal by inheritance nor by their environment, and when the school attempts to set the same standards for all children, it is flying in the face of reason. We must set our standards of achievement in terms of the capacities of the individual—and this is done very rarely in the typical school. This is not entirely the fault of the school systems. The schools are like a child who has been sent to do a man's work. We have teachers who are burdened with forty or fifty children in a class, and a teacher in that situation *keeps* school; she cannot *teach* school. Overemphasis on the academic curriculum is criticized today; manual training is clearly more appropriate for many pupils who are now forced to take *academics* or leave school.

We may be in danger of total catastrophe in our schools because the children are not being reached individually. The reports of indiscipline are increasing every day; policemen have to be stationed in schools; and the result is a learning climate which is nothing short of disgraceful for this richest country in the world. The question is not whether we can afford to have good schools, the question is whether we can afford *not* to have good schools.

Lee Harvey Oswald is an example of one who early showed overt hostility. He was taken to a child guidance clinic by his mother, but she failed to follow through on the counseling given her. Lee grew up a hostile loner. The Marine Corps found that he was more of a liability than an asset and permanently discharged him. Then, perhaps in order *to be somebody* he proceeded to assassinate our President. The tragedy in Oswald's case is that countless other children are being reared in even less desirable homes as regards security, love, and wholesome living and school conditions. We are continuing to *spawn* social misfits such as Oswald. Their cost will be astronomical.

The school (See Chapter X) becomes an intolerable place for many children and they respond by running away from it. It is too painful for them to endure. They cannot stand to have other children laugh at their poor progress. Peer group influence, as previously noted, is responsible for shaping behavior more than anything else. Youngsters do not worry about teachers, parents, or even policemen; they *do* obey and fear—very greatly—the children of their own social group.

Truancy is an indication of the failure of the schools to meet the needs of children. It is related in part to the poor home background that some of these children come from: an environment where education is not prized, where the models they see are those who are *making it* in drugs, vice, gambling, and other crimes. The whole example they see is negative as far as social values are concerned. In the ghetto, criminals are often the *generals* in their society,, not the failures.

Children learn early that if they throw themselves on the floor and kick and scream for an ice cream cone, the mother runs and gets a dime for them—so they continue this pattern. The reinforcement they get from their behavior is such that they continue to manife'st it. This requires, certainly, that mothers must be taught better child-rearing practices. The tantrums described above are an early indication of the acting out violence that seriously maladjusted children show. The child growing up where standards of reasonable behavior were not set and required and who finds he can achieve satisfaction by deviant behavior, will continue it.

Early inability to get along with others is a criterion noticed immediately by teachers, social workers, and others who handle juvenile pre-delinquents. A tendency is shown by disturbed youths to force the external world to conform to the individual rather than for the individual to conform to the external world. This is an alarming indication of psychotic behavior or of severe neurotic behavior. If the child is in a home where unreasonable standards of conformity are set, where there is rigidity, where there is frequent corporal punishment, where the child feels insecure, helpless and unwanted, obviously he will not develop patterns of behavior that will enable him to get along with others. Now, we must question whether such children would be considered normal. We know there is going to be some mild indication of all these traits, but where they become marked, where the behavior is obviously odd, then clearly some therapy, some search for understanding of the behavior is indicated.

Can such abnormal behavior be handled within the family?

It is almost hopeless to expect that it can be handled within the family unless the family has been given some help by way of prior educational opportunity to learn something about human behavior and human relations. In a home where there is illiteracy, where the mother is an alcoholic or an addict, or where there is a succession of *uncles* living in the home (the father having long since abandoned the family), it is futile to expect that the parents can do much by way of therapy for deviant behavior. This situation is found very often in minority ethnic and lower socio-economic classes. Here the school must again extend its resources to cover this unmet need to teach mental hygiene, citizenship and ethical character.

Home visitation by the social worker is desirable. If the mothers could be persuaded to come to a class, perhaps held at night, where they could learn something about home economics, family planning, dietetics, personal and mental hygiene, and child psychology, the present deplorable situation could be, in time, improved. For example, if mothers would learn just the one simple fact that children under the age of two or two-and one-half do not have sphincter control and cannot voluntarily control bladder and bowel functions, many children might be saved from beatings and even death because they become wet or are soiled. Just a little knowledge of physiology is needed, so that the mother would understand that she is expecting something from the child which he cannot control until he has physically matured enough to have this voluntary control over the sphincter muscle.

On a long-range basis, we know how this can be handled and should be handled—that is, by having a first-class educational system everywhere; children would be given education for day-in and day-out living. For example, sex education should be given during the elementary school years, when sexual experimentation begins. We must get away from the prudish idea that children in junior high school are not going to get pregnant or contract VD. We know that they do become pregnant—thousands do, and VD is epidemic among youths. Somehow the school must teach these fundamental facts of life, since it seems the home, and church, and non-school agencies are ineffective in too many instances at all levels of society. It does not matter much whether a child can spell if he doesn't understand the basic facts of life such as personal hygiene, sexual functioning, and some insights into interpersonal and intra-personal human relations—mental hygiene.

The family itself must have an emotional climate of security, support, affection, respect, and discipline, which will enable the child to come to school and to learn efficiently. Too many children are on the streets until midnight, go to school without breakfast, and have no one to care whether they have clean clothes to wear or a bath every day. We must somehow mobilize our total resources across the board for physical care, health care, and emotional and mental care. Our children deserve better.

The immediate need on the part of the family would be to have an intervention of ideas by visitation counselors, who would concentrate on such simple things as just making sure that a child gets to bed at night by a reasonable hour on school nights; that non-school hours are supervised by some responsible adult. The family must be sensitized to the fact that great harm and trouble is in store unless each child is treated as someone who is important and is given proper supervision and care.

Where the home has fallen apart so completely that this supervision is impossible, even with the help of social services, then certainly a foster home or institutional care is the only other answer. Much more use should be made of foster homes in preference to institutional care. Environmental manipulation in some cases must be resorted to. The child must be taken out of an environment where he is destined to become a prison statistic, into one where he has some hope of adjustment.

When overt hostility regretably results in a police charge, the matter is brought out into the open. If the family cannot handle the child, he must be handled by others with more capability. A child who is incorrigible, who is a delinquent, who is a run-away, must somehow be controlled. If this means institutional confinement, reluctantly then this must follow.

Where intervention is clearly indicated it must be implemented. To hope that troublesome cases will spontaneously get better is a serious misconception; they usually get worse unless treated.

Individual violence occurs almost invariably at a stress point where something has triggered off the violent behavior. The violence is an acting-out in the face of a frustration, of a block to some satisfaction, or there has been a build-up of anxiety of a compulsive nature and the normal controls have failed at that moment. There is a heavy emotional coloration of the episode. We must bear in mind that we think emotionally—we don't think with the whole brain. We think with the hind brain, the old brain. The forebrain, which is a more recent acquisition of mankind, functions when we are calm and collected. But when we *lose our cool* (and we actually do lose it, because the temperature goes up) *condition red* happens. There is sweating, rapid heart beat, deeper breathing, more sugar in the blood stream, the whole physiological reaction of condition red which accompanies anger. Violent behavior is related to anger and to fear. The triggering of this can be by a very mild stimulus, or it may take a tremendous concentration of stimuli to bring the individual to the flash point. Violent behavior is a blind striking out, where people use their hands or use instruments to hurt or kill.

Violent behavior is sick behavior. The individual, after the violent episode, will usually have regret, but not always. Some psychotic individuals can take a life and have no remorse. These are totally psychopathic, sociopathic individuals. But the violent episode which has a pattern of occuring, shows that the individual has been using this as his solution. This is his *modus operandi* and he seizes upon it as a solution when he finds other alternative solutions are not available to him. He will then strike out in desperation.

In order to prevent a pattern of violent behavior, we have to try somehow, particularly in early childhood, to condition children that violence is evil, that it is counter-productive, that it does more harm than good, that it does not solve any problems, that it is often irreversible and may cause permanent harm. It is an unbelievable animal reaction which man manifests. This requires a whole reshaping relation to our childhood, adulthood, and an understanding of what drugs and alcohol will do to release inhibitions and make possible violent, vicious, depraved behavior. This is what happens when an individual acts under the blind stimulation of fear, anger, lust or drugs. He acts on a *gut-level* basis—and the results are often nothing short of catastrophic.

In this connection, incrimination (correlation) of violence on TV with violent acting-out behavior by some children is accepted as a plausible theory by social psychologists today.

Although any one-to-one correlation of heredity and criminal behavior in a particular case is clearly not possible, it is believed that genetically influenced variables may exert a *thrust toward criminality*, according to Dr. David Rosenthal of the National Institute of Mental Health.[1] Brain wave abnormalities, associated with bad judgment and poor impulse control; low I.Q.; mesomorphic body build, with low tolerance of frustration and poor ego control; psychotic and pre-psychotic behavior, related to a genetic factor; chromosomal abnormality manifested in psychological distress and personality disturbance; alcoholism and drug addiction with an inherited predisposing factor; homosexual behavior, related to genetic factor; and hyperactive children with inherited factor, are recognized as shaping forces which affect behavior, whether criminal or non-criminal in manifestation. This is not the same as saying criminals are born to be that way; rather, it is to admit that genetic factors must be considered as part of the nature-nurture combination already discussed in this chapter.

[1] National Institutes of Mental Health, Laboratory of Psychology, Bethesda, Md., News Release, *Chicago Daily News*, 1972.

CHAPTER X

THE PUBLIC SCHOOL

IN CONTEMPORARY AMERICA, the school is a social institution in serious trouble. The twelve-year educational ladder, which begins at ages five to six and ends for most at sixteen to seventeen, is in need of revitalization and redirection, with a massive infusion of public concern and support. Our schools seem to have lost their sense of direction. The 1917 goals[1] were the command of the fundamental processes (the 3 R's), health, worthy home membership, development of ethical character, worthy use of leisure time, vocational training, and citizenship. Later international understanding was added as an objective. In 1972, one in every three Americans was in school.

Today, *caving-in* by school administrators, unconcern and disinterest by many parents, attacks on the schools by *economy-first* reactionary groups who think first of saving tax money and last about quality education, outright despair by some teachers, and vicious militancy by a few teachers and disaffected and deluded youths of school age, have created a critical situation. Cities are closing schools early because of money shortages and assignment of police officers is required for keeping order in many inner-city schools. Teenage girls brazenly demand the right to go braless, alleging an invasion of their *rights*, and boys with hair below their shoulders defy controls by the school authorities, who, more often than not, fail to take any corrective action. In short, a complete breakdown of the traditional school as it

[1] *The Seven Cardinal Principles of Secondary Education.* United States Office of Education, 1917.

has existed for over one hundred years in this country is threatened.

In this context, it is necessary to note some glaring deficiencies which the school has allowed to develop:

1. The school has not fitted to the child. It has usually forced all students to take a standard curriculum which does not relate to the needs and abilities of many. It is a *word* school rather than a *doing* school. It has regarded all children as equally able to learn—a great error. Children *learn by doing,* Professor John Dewey wisely stated about a hundred years ago. Yet our schools rarely have vocational training which is related to the world outside the school, and many pupils drop out because the traditional curriculum does not relate to their needs as they see them. Some ninety percent of prison inmates are school drop-outs.

2. The schools do not identify, diagnose, and treat children with problems. Counseling at a crossroad of a life can salvage many children who have educational, behavioral, and personal prolems; neglected, such children are destined for serious trouble. Children must be evaluated as they progress on the basis of their own individual capacities, not according to some arbitrary expectations applicable to a few.

3. The schools are institutions in the total sense of the word: impersonal, authoritarian, rigid, mechanical, and always years behind the times. For example, today's drug abuse, venereal disease, and illegitimate births, are out of control, in part because the schools failed to see these impending changes and did not cope with them effectively years ago at the start. One should not blame the schools for all these problems, but the schools surely are implicated in part for them. Society deserves the schools it gets, because it accepts them.

4. Public support for free education for *all the children of the people* has never been adequate. Dual system education for whites and blacks has been costly and has brought up generations of blacks and browns who have had inferior quality schools—this cannot be

denied. Integrated schools with small minority proportions have been functioning successfully in the North
for generations. To suddenly integrate, by bussing, in
areas in which heavy proportions are black, or brown,
has created another grave problem threatening tax support for the schools. Some school districts are voting
down building programs, and better school programs,
where such needs are clearly justified. The ultimate
costs of such short-sighted social actions will be great.
There can be little doubt that there is a direct connection
between level of financial input, pupils' socio-economic
status, the quality of school service available, pupils'
performance, and post-school achievement. The ability
of a local school district to generate revenue from property taxes should not be allowed to serve as the primary
determinant of the quality of school services it offers
to children.

5. The curriculum must be up-dated to cover sex education,
    drug abuse, social problems, health (V.D.) and personal
    deportment (needed especially for children from
    broken homes). The pervasive and destructive influ-
    ences of violence and distortions of reality on television
    must be countered by sensitivity training, readings, and
    involvement between persons who care. The ghetto
    of the inner city with its social asphyxia must somehow
    be redirected with hope and opportunity, including bet-
    ter jobs and housing.

6. Where a child lives should not be the determining factor
    in the quality of his education; ignorance cannot be
    quarantined—the *un-people* move from their ghetto sur-
    roundings to other areas, and take with them their
    ignorance, superstitions, and hostilities. Recent tax
    reform proposals seek to ease the burden on property
    owners for school tax support. The goal should be to
    tax the money needed for schools where the tax base
    is, for children where they are. The present tax system
    is clearly unfair and inadequate, with the suburbs able
    to afford better schools with less tax load than the inner
    city.

The school has been called the place where we polish the brickbats and dull the diamonds. To learn should be a natural and happy activity for children, as it is for monkeys. Unfortunately for many children, the school *turns them off* or makes *pushouts* by its methods and materials for learning. The child is confirmed in his self-image of unworthiness. The self-fulfilling prophecy of many pupils and teachers often results in a child making lesser progress. Too many teachers and parents expect too little progress from children who have built-in handicaps of poor home environment, absence of enriching experiences, poor school equipment and staff (as goes the teacher, so goes the school), and uninspired school authorities who are content with pedestrian quality of the teaching system.

The school itself contributes to poor mental hygiene for many children by its unreasonable expectations of progress, failure to adjust to individual differences, and rejection of many children who do not readily conform to hypothetical *norms*.

Mental maturity testing (I.Q.) is subject to many limitations of reliability or validity. Its findings must be interpreted in terms of whether the test is culturally fair. *I.Q.* tests based on reading are reading tests, not valid tests of mental maturity.

A school is a lot of books with a few people around to help get something out of the books. The library is the beating heart of every school. Children must be taught to read and then they must be motivated to read. Books are the oldest and best *teaching machines*.

The school is the *business* of adolescents. How the school does its job is critical to social progress and delinquency control. Ghetto schools must have superior staffs and faculties to off-set the deficiencies for learning which exist there. Society's problem is not whether we can afford good schools, the question is whether we can afford *not* to have good schools.

Whether public support for non-public (parochial or private) schools will develop is not clear at this time. Parochial schools are in grave financial trouble. Many feel that some subsidy is justified, but constitutional provisions which require separation of church and state forbid such help at this time by the Federal Government.

Little doubt exists that there is a direct connection between money spent for schools, the socio-economic status (home environment), quality of school program, and the achievement of pupils both in school and post-school. Education should be a life-long process. The unfavorable impoverished home environment of many pupils is recognized today as a grave handicap in life's race for success, for it often entails psychological settings of poor motivation and reduced expectations.

In many of the nation's largest cities, half or more of the pupils are non-white and preponderantly poor. One out of every three drops out of high school and the average pupil who stays in school is two years behind the national reading norms. Many teachers and pupils live in constant fear of robbery or injury from physical assault; police officers must patrol many inner-city schools to protect teachers and pupils. *Compensatory* education—designed to offset the built-in cultural disadvantages of ghetto children—has been widely judged to be a failure. Performance contracting, involving contracts between private companies and school board authorities, has recently been judged to be less than a success, another failure in a long list of innovations which have marked the history of education, especially since the 1930's and the so-called *progressive education* of that era which attempted on theoretically sound ground to fit the school to the child and to adjust expectations of school achievement to the capacities of each child.

The plain facts are that the deprived and segregated environments of millions of culturally deprived children destine them to poor academic progress and to early drop-out. These children will be the rejects in a future draft call-up (in World War II, one out of every three was rejected), will be last hired and first fired in employment shifts, and will comprise our prison, relief, and non-paying hospital case loads. A *tax-eating* status is a certainty for most of them. How long can a democracy survive with such long-term costly liabilities clearly inevitable unless the present collision course with social disaster is averted? A total mobilization of the nation's resources is imperatively needed to cope with the imminent disintegration of today's society. Each year the picture is less favorable and time is clearly running out, in the opinion of many governmental and sociological authorities.[2]

Relative to Unit 12, Racism—The Ghetto, the desperate financial plight of some twenty-five to thirty of our largest cities demands imperative attention. If their schools go under, how can the cities themselves survive? Dr. Mark Shedd,[3] former Superintendent of the Philadelphia Public Schools, suggests a massive infusion of Federal money under a policy of nationalization of big city schools. The cities, in his view, simply do not get their fair share of tax receipts. The money is in the suburbs, he points out, not in the cities where the need is greatest.

Apparently we have a choice between supporting public education as it must be supported, or of pouring infinitely greater sums of money into a police state tomorrow. The loss of human potential—which is the greatest waste of any natural resource—with its concurrent tragedy of escalating welfare costs, crime, and social asphyxia is directly related to ineffective schools.

Introduction to psychology (general psychology) is an excellent subject for senior high schools; some two hundred Ohio high schools are offering it (1972). The insights from this subject are greatly needed by adolescents and they are as fully capable of studying it as college freshmen.

Mental maturity tests have long been criticized on the grounds that they are not *culture-fair*—they fit relatively well only to Western, white middle-class children for which they were designed. Black, or Mexican-American children are clearly at a disadvantage in such testing. Children put in *retarded* classes are often found to be misassigned, and are able to do regular class work.

For linguistically impoverished children—those who are reading at several grade levels below their chronological or school age cohorts—school is a self-annihilating experience.

[2] *Newsweek*, April 3, 1972, p. 50.
[3] Quoted in *The Christian Science Monitor*, March 4, 1972, p. 13.

They are shamed, humiliated, and condemned to continued academic failure as they move by *automatic* promotion along the hostile educational ladder. All schools are basically reading schools. Reading skills should be the heart of the curriculum. Poor readers are destined to fail, to drop out, and fill an inferior life position. It is estimated that two and one-half million Americans have reading handicaps, and that over eighteen million adults cannot read well enough to fill out *survival forms*—applications for Social Security, drivers' licenses, Medicare, or bank loans.

A great fault of many schools is that the teacher talks too much, the children talk too little. Some ninety percent of the talking should be by the children; the teacher does not need *recitation* practice. Children will *learn to do by doing* as Professor John Dewey taught at the turn of the century, not by being *talked-at* by the teacher. Our Armed Forces in World War II used multi-sensory aids as the method of teaching; they *kept the talk short.* The pattern of instruction, with emphasis on the *doings* was *Tell them how, show them how, and have them do it.* Passive learning is not good learning; the learner must be active and involved in *finding out.* Schools can be exciting places of discovery. That they are not, that children are *turned off* is a great fault of some of today's mechanized impersonal schools, frequently found in inner-city areas. Misguided school boards which cut support for guidance counselors and special education teachers in economy actions are surely compounding delinquency and life adjustment problems for future great costs to society.

First in the educational process should be the assignment of teachers who are psychologically adjusted and emotionally sensitized to working in an environment where slow, sometimes hostile, students are the rule and not the exception. This would facilitate mutual trust and understanding. Secondly, programs should be developed to place the student in classes that are adjusted to his learning capabilities. This would accelerate his feelings of security and almost negate defeatist attitudes. There should be more emphasis on teaching the student to survive in a middle-class society by placing more emphasis on teaching trades and the sociological and psychological mores of the society in which he must live. The language and accents of the majority social class must be taught if employment is to be expected in today's working America. So-called *black studies* contribute little to job placement or success. This is a *reality* of life today.

Discipline is necessary if a stable learning environment is to exist in our schools. Unfortunately, methods used to this end have traditionally been negative in nature. Corporal punishment has, for the most part, been replaced by suspension practices. These practices, while they do temporarily remove a problem from the school, have manifold adverse aspects. Disruptive or habitually truant students are the least likely ones able to afford a further void in their educational experiences although they usually welcome the vacation. Lack of supervision by parents increases the possibility of the suspended student's becoming involved in delinquencies within the community at large. Resentment resulting from the suspension action may result in retaliation against the school or teachers. Late in 1972, in one of the nation's largest cities, two suspended boys set a fire causing $90,000 in school damage. More effort must be directed by the schools toward providing more positive means of maintaining discipline, thus avoiding shortcomings inherent in the exclusive employment of negative reinforcement measures.

Very few school districts provide ongoing education for pregnant girls. They are treated as contaminated outcasts and are banned from the campus when their pregnancy becomes evident. These girls are penalized at least a year of their education and most never return to regain the lost educational opportunity. Girls who become permanent drop-outs can be expected to contribute significantly to the surging welfare rolls. Ongoing education must be provided if these young girls are to be prepared to become contributing members of society.

Until the public realizes the crucial importance of the public school as the great (but not the only) shaping force it is, and gives the school as a social institution the means to do the tremendous task assigned to it, the waste of our most precious natural resource—our children—will continue its dismal course with social disintegration the inevitable consequence. Time is rapidly running out; in fact, we may already have passed the point of no return in this fatal direction and the salvaging of our present society may be in doubt. Clearly, broadside emergency efforts to rescue the schools are imperatively needed.

CHAPTER XI

PERSONALITY THEORIES

PERSONALITY IS DEFINED as an individual's dynamic behavior
system stemming from his conscious and unconscious life
space perceptions. Allport's definition is perhaps the best
known:

> Personality is the dynamic organization within the individual of
> those psychophysical systems that determine his characteristic
> behavior and thought . . . Personality *is* something and *does* some-
> thing . . . it is what lies *behind* specific acts and *within* the
> individual.[1]

Personality is rough hewn by heredity and shaped and
refined by the environment. The early years are of the greatest
importance since the personality is most plastic and malleable
at that time; later reshaping of the personality is always possible, but at great cost of time and effort. The human personality appears to be melted and reshaped anew during the adolescent period.

There are a number of personality theories which attempt
to explain human behavior: behaviorism (John B. Watson),
connectionism (E.L. Thorndike), classical conditioning (I.P.
Pavlov), operant conditioning (B.F. Skinner), psychoanalytic
(Sigmund Freud), neo-Freudian (Karen Horney), self-theory
(Carl Rogers), and existential psychology (Heidegger). The
Neo-Freudians insist upon the relevance of social psychologi-
cal variables against the strong instinctive views of the
Freudians.

Each of these theoretical positions has merit and deserves
consideration at the reader's leisure; we will briefly survey
herein the views of Doctors Freud and Skinner.

[1] Allport, G.: Quoted in Hall and Lindsey: *Theories of Personality*, p. 263.

The role of conscious memory as shaper of conscious behavior is undoubtedly important. Dream life, free reverie, hypnotic behavior, accidents of living, slips of the tongue, doodling, electric stimulation of brain areas, sleepwalking, foregetfulness (e.g., dental appointments), multiple personality, parapraxes, and sudden insightful solutions to problems, all have relationship to unconscious mental processes.

Sigmund Freud, M.D. (1856–1939) said of himself that he did not believe he was a great man, but he did believe that he had made a great discovery: the world of the unconscious. He postulated that all impressions (learnings and experiences) which we gain from living are recorded in our memory and cannot be cancelled out. All is received, classified, stored, and retrieved by the twelve billion or so cells of the brain. We are shaped from earliest infancy by the process of living. This subtle and insidious process goes on without our being aware of its operation. The feedback from experience of living, with some behavior rewarded and strengthened and some punished and inhibited, is what molds and conditions our personality. Dr. Freud believed in the significance of mental factors in the different vital functions as well as in illnesses and their treatment, and that sex played a great part in personality shaping, with fixations on parental figures (the father for girls, the mother for boys) which he called the Oedipal relationship or *family romance.*

Since sexual outlets are controlled by customs and laws, a great deal of frustration and conflict accompanies it. Trauma (shocks) from sexual experiences in early life are often related to later emotional maladjustments and even to serious mental illness, in Freud's view. Psychodynamic processes involving the unconscious are involved in creative thinking, artistic production, and religious experience.

Freud said there were three levels of personality: *id* (primitive urges); *ego* (reality principle); and *super-ego* (conscience). He believed the task of the psychotherapist was to bring to the conscious level that which is unconscious, and that mental illness could be treated by deep analysis of the unconscious levels of personality. He said there was both a life instinct and a death instinct which operates in all persons. He developed theories of dream analysis with both latent (hidden) and manifest (apparent) aspects, and interpreted the symbols found in dreams; dreams were indications of wish-fulfillment of deep unconscious needs.

Hypnosis as a therapeutic tool was abandoned by Freud because the patient does not remember what happens during hypnotic sleep. Freud wanted the patient to help with his own treatment, which is a requirement in all psychotherapy.

For Freud, conflict and frustration are the name of the game for humans, and this means that some mental illness for some people is to be regarded as an inevitable consequence of living. We have physical, psychological, and cultural barriers which thwart expressions of personality. When these blocks are not resolved or are not effectively adjusted to, hostility, aggression, sexual difficulties, and both psychological and physiological stress inevitably results. Every individual has a *breaking point* which cannot be passed without physical or emotional damage. The end process is a psychological casualty functioning inefficiently in life's struggle, or even in the closed ward of a mental hospital.

Dr. Freud formulated theories relative to the oral, anal, phallic, latent, and genital periods of human sexual development and their psychological implications. You are invited to read his perceptive writings.

Aggression has been given much importance by Freud, as expressed directly, by physical or verbal assaults, or indirectly (vicariously) as in watching boxing. Hostility toward authority, compulsive theft, suicide, battered child syndrome, sexual assaults, murder, contact sports, hunting, spectator sports such as bull-fighting, punching a bag, are all related to deep personality traits and reflect destructive forces of instinctive nature. Their dynamic power to shape human behavior is evident.

Anxiety is defined as a psychophysical reaction to threat; it is a sign of danger which the individual then uses to initiate adjustment countermeasures to restore equilibrium. Some anxiety is *free-floating* without reference to a specific cause. Anxiety is both a cause of physical stress and can result from it, with inescapable somatic involvement of glandular, muscular, and visceral organs. The executive's gastric ulcer is an example of a psychogenic illness.

Birth trauma is the first anxiety-provoking threat experienced by the individual. Anxiety is a symptom used by mentally ill persons, and has utility for them. They get secondary gain from their symptom and the symptom serves a purpose: to gain attention, sympathy, excuse from work, and to mask the real basic underlying stress factor causing the symptom. Treating the symptom and removing it will not cure the basic causal factor. The symptom may be a useful defense which the patient employs unconsciously to excuse or to rationalize out of his present impasse situation. Anxiety is the basic symptom for all emotional disorders.

Guilt and anxiety are related, and the dynamic consequences of both are stress reactions involving both physical and psychological aspects of behavior. *Condition red* which is a generalized physiological response to fear, rage, or love, involves the entire body (soma). The polygraph's operation with the autonomic nervous system's independent working exemplifies this physical response. The psychological response to severe and chronic anxiety is depression and disintegration of personality, with both emotional and physical evidences (e.g., depression, insomnia, indigestion).

Trauma in the form of death, temporary separations, hospitalization, weaning, entering school, marriage, and family terminal disintegration are anxiety-provoking for all persons.

Guilt, in the form of self-blame, is inevitable for all of us. We fail both by omission and commission as we pass along life's trials from birth to death. Guilt involves fantasy, and introspection, with remorse, regrets, and self-incrimination, often with no useful purpose to be served. The role of confession as a safety valve for guilt is recognized. Suicide has a guilt aspect which is overladen with hostility, even to the point of self-destruction.

Freud formulated the following defense mechanisms which are useful as adjustments (not solutions) against guilt and anxiety: repression, substitution, rationalization, projection, illness (escape by), regression, identification, compensation, sublimation, reaction formation, and fantasy.

Freud's original thinking and restatement of other thinking in a new context is shown in the theoretical and technical innovations which flowed from such concepts as the following:

The Dynamic Unconscious
Transference
Narcissism
Resistance
Rationalization
Symptom Formation—The symptoms of illness can be shown to serve the unconscious needs of the patient.
The Neurotic Conflict
Fixation
Conversion
Displacement
Object Relationships—Cathexis
Dream Analysis—The dreamer often expresses in his dreams wishes of which he is unaware, on a level of full awareness.
Libido
Freudian Slips of the Tongue (Parapraxes)
Life and Death Instincts
Pleasure Principle—Immediate gratification
Reality Principle—Deferred gratification
Repression—Need to "ventilate" the unconscious

You are invited to read Freud's works or any standard text in abnormal psychology for elaboration of the above.

Id—biological, primary, primitive, elemental animal impulses; reservoir of instinctual urges, basic, unrefined, and unbridled drives, such as lust and aggression, a seething cauldron of vicious hedonistic passions hidden deep within the core of personality. *Id* operates on the pleasure principle, and is present at birth. It interacts with *ego* and *superego,* if and when it can circumvent them. The *id* is the repository of selfish instincts, but if there were no taboos there would be no gratifications; hence, we now have some gratification for all, but not all for some.

Ego—the reality principle, the executive and social component of the personality; it perceives, thinks, feels, and does, and takes a stand against the pleasure seeking of the *id*. Parents use guilt and punishment to control children; this is reality.

Superego—the conscience; the internalization of all the external controls that play upon the individual. It is *grown* at home, from earliest conditioning by *feedback* from intrafamily interaction: The mother's role is crucial. Some individuals are lacking in all superego controls; they are the product of a loveless rearing.

The mind can be likened to an iceberg; the smaller part above the surface is the region of consciousness, the much larger mass below water is the region of the unconscious: urges, passions, the repressed ideas and feelings, the great underworld of vital, unseen forces which exercise an imperious control over the conscious thoughts and acts of man.

Freud's theory is one explanation, among others, in studying the behavior of man. He was such an intellectual giant that all who follow him in a sense *ape* him and must use much of his terminology. Freud's theory tries to envisage man as an animal beset with instinctual drives, living in a hostile world, with reason not a basis for life; man is in the predicament of knowing, as no other animal does, that he must die. Freud postulated that the etiology of mental illness must be discovered in order to achieve its therapy (abreaction, catharsis).

At the other swing of the pendulum of behavior theory, and with diametric opposite position, is Dr. B.F. Skinner, perhaps the most influential American psychologist of recent times. Known as operant (instrumental) reinforcement theory, its central idea is that when behavior which is wanted appears, it is to be reinforced with immediate reward. The animal (human or infra-human) does something and gets something. In contrast to Pavlovian classical conditioning, where the dog either salivated or did not, the experimental subject in the *Skinner Box* is active and has a choice of several possible behaviors.The specific behavior which is desired is *paid off* promptly when it is manifested. Skinner believes man's life is now *programmed* by external controls, and the best good for all will be a world where social controls will be designed to reward behavior which is good for society: freedom, as now experienced in the western world, will be lost to a pattern of life like the *discipline* of Red China. Behavior is shaped and maintained by its consequences, he maintains. A strict behavioristic psychologist, he accords no place to depth factors of personality, instincts, or *inner life* of cognitive processes. Environments are defective when they fail to make desirable behavior pay off or when they resort primarily to revengeful punishment as a means of deterring or stopping undesirable behavior.

Mental hospitals, schools, governments (Red China notably), have used Skinnerian reinforcement to shape behavior in directions desired, with effective results. Operant conditioning brings many forms of behavior under stimulus control, for deliberate manipulation toward a desired goal. The possibility exists that human society may indeed be transformed by widespread application of this social theory. Its negative aspects, a *World of 1984* with individual freedoms sharply restricted, institutional living for the *masses* and *big brother* computerized controls penetrating every facet of life, makes one pause in fear as this possibility becomes more likely as time passes. Whether the *family* as we now conceive it will survive is not certain.

CHAPTER XII

RACISM—THE GHETTO

SOCIOLOGISTS HAVE FOR centuries observed the phenomenon of the movement of city dwellers who can afford to do so from the inner-city to more livable and esthetically pleasant suburban areas. This movement has made available the living quarters of those who have moved; these abandoned quarters were usually in run-down condition and near factories and railroad yards.

Overcrowding was at once the norm and the tenement or slum was born. Landlords subdivided the brownstone front mansions into apartments and rooms with some sleeping areas occupied by as many as three sleepers in the same bed, for eight hours each. Immigrants from Europe had no choice but to pay exhorbitant rents for these miserable accommodations.

In time, the white Europeans were supplanted by blacks from the southeastern part of the country. The same overcrowded and deplorable conditions of squalor have continued to this day in the so-called target area, the ghettos of our great cities. The poor are, in fact, incarcerated in our central cities.

The ghettos of all cities show the same characteristics: abandoned, rundown buildings, dirty, odorous, rat-infested, overcrowded, noisy, and crime-ridden. The line of demarcation from the slum to the more prosperous areas is usually clearly defined. At night, the ghetto becomes a no-man's land of fear and terror, with crime rates perhaps ten times as great as in the suburbs. People living in the ghetto form eighty per cent of the victims of crime there, and this means, usually, blacks preying upon blacks, since most ghetto residents are blacks. Daily figures for homicides, burglaries, assaults, and robberies are appalling. Police power is rarely effective in the ghetto after dark, and police are effectively barred from entering some ghetto areas during non-daylight hours; it becomes *enemy territory* for police.

The ghetto is the habitat of the *un-people*—the unemployed, unhealthy, unhappy, unstable, unclean, unmotivated, and unwanted. It is the last stopping place for the alcoholics, addicts, and sociopaths who cannot make it in the open world. It is a sub-culture with its own language, social norms and philosophy of life. Police, probation, and welfare officers unfamiliar with its way of life must be sensitized to its peculiar mores and standards, or lack of standards.

For youths raised in this more criminogenic milieu, the prognosis for their involvement in delinquency is many times higher than that for children living in affluent and hygienic neighborhoods where the differential of environmental shaping is more favorable.

Police-public relations are almost impossible to achieve on a viable basis. Residents in the ghetto hate because they fear the police; they fear because they do not understand; and they do not understand because they do not communicate—according to U.S. Representative Walter Fauntroy of Washington, D.C.[1] He further observed that the ghetto residents do not believe they get adequate police protection, that the police neglect them, and that there is police brutality—born of fear. He added that the polarization of whites versus blacks, of rich versus poor, of city versus suburban, is reflected among police department personnel.

Inner-city residents look upon the police with mixed emotions; yet, paradoxically, these residents need more police protection and should support the police fully with information about criminal activity, assistance to police in case of difficult arrest (often there is interference by the mob, not help for the police, even when a vicious junkie is seized by the police). The problem to be solved is how to improve communications to reduce fear and hate. Needed in this connection are:

[1] Remarks made at the American Psychological Association meeting, September 5, 1971, Washington, D.C.

1. Increased proportions of minority groups in law inforcement. This is difficult since many applicants are poorly educated, of inferior physique, and police employment is not attractive to them (their friends call them *Uncle Toms*).
2. Emphasis upon sensitivity training for those who police (occupy) the inner city, in order to prepare officers to cope with special ethnic cultures and languages.
3. Establishment of working relations with community leaders (block leaders) in ghetto areas.
4. Police efforts are needed to project a better image and to counter false allegations made by enemies of law and order. News media must be provided with positive, factual news to abort false rumors which anti-social persons are always ready to circulate. Police involvement with boys clubs, athletics, and school liaison is needed.

Negro leaders have charged that field interrogations are predominately conducted in slum communities, that they are used indiscriminately and that they are conducted in an abusive and unfriendly manner. The police claim they are trying to be fair. They, too, feel that police brutality, abuse of authority, and discourteous behavior, especially when they are unpunished, not only constitute a serious threat to community support of the police, but also undermine the citizens respect for law enforcement agencies and for the law itself.

The ghetto is a system of poverty, ignorance, hate, superstition, violence, fear, and resistance against the restraints of the *square* world. The word *repression* is often heard; residents feel oppressed, defeated, and programmed for a continued life of want and deprivation. Many have succumbed to their seemingly hopeless predicament and cease to help themselves. This fact is a partial explanation for the continued presence of a critical mix of hatred and violence which is always latent in the ghetto and which flashes into a river of hate when any incident occurs which upsets, even briefly, normal police controls—such as a riot, natural disaster, or a violent mass protest march. Perhaps the most alarming fact is that many ghetto residents have lost faith in the government as protector and provider. Housing is still the national scandal it has been for years; schools are more turbulent; and rates of crime, unemployment, disease, and heroin addiction are higher each year. Welfare rolls are larger.

If poor blacks and Mexican-Americans continue, as is most likely, to be isolated in ghettos, most cities by 1980 will be largely ghettos of minority racial origin. It is apparent that the priorities of the nation must be reordered. We are indeed on a razor edge of decision whether our society will be split into two societies, one white, the other black, separate and unequal, with great harm and danger to both as the result. In the three years since the Kerner Report warned of this imminent danger, little has been done to change conditions in the face of this ominous prediction threatening national disaster. Time is running out to effect obvious corrections for the malaise of society: a mobilization across the board, comparable to that for war, must be mounted, to level the ghettos, provide job training, employment, good education for both children and adults, better medical care, recreation, public transportation, welfare assistance (for those unable to work, and for whom jobs exist), decent housing (*not* the vertical city instant slum), and most of all, hope for a better life for the millions who exist in the teeming hovels of our inner-city areas. Unless they have some stake in society, conformity to laws is meaningless for many. Yet, the fact must be faced that many of these people do not do for themselves those essential services which government cannot do: for example, putting garbage out in cans with a cover for pickup, rather than throwing it in hallways of housing projects. People rehabilitation must accompany property rehabilitation.

The police, as the bearing edge of society, have a most difficult role in interaction with ghetto residents. Police and firemen are targets for snipers, assaulters, and ambushers. Unless society revises its attitudes and treatment of the police, personnel recruitment for police work will be virtually impossible. Police corruption, as recently charged in New York City and Philadelphia, will always be a possibility, particularly where police pay is not adequate to cope with inflation, a common condition in today's economy.

Conditions of black, teen-age employment in the ghettos that helped spark the 1967 racial riots appear to be less favorable, with perhaps half unemployed. Prejudices still exist. The underlying social problems have not been solved or even ameliorated, and the machinery of law enforcement is breaking down, in the opinion of former Attorney General Katzenbach:

> It seems to me that the country faces a choice, that with the increase in crime we are either going to put the resources in incorporating the kind of recommendations that this report has to improve police, courts, correctional process, or we are going to have more and more in the way of repression. Because people are not going to tolerate the kind of crime rate that we have, and we are going to solve it the right way—which is the hard way—or we are going to have more and more repression in our society.[2]

Thomas Jefferson, some two hundred years ago, warned that the danger to America's destruction would come from the great cities. His prediction seems about to come true: unless great efforts are made to abort this threat, most of our great cities by 1980 will be largely black and brown, and totally bankrupt.

A phenomenon of the late sixties and early seventies has been the so-called *youth ghettos,* notably at Berkeley, California, and at Madison, Wisconsin. These enclaves comprise large numbers of dropouts, hide-outs, students, anti-establishment types, *street people,* AWOLS, runaways, drug freaks, and some vicious criminals. Here only certain laws are enforced, and only certain styles of living are accepted. Hostility and non-cooperation with the *square world* are central themes. Free health clinics, cooperative stores, a central mess, and a way of life best characterized as *counter-culture* apparently define these relatively new-type ghettos. Their viability is fragile.

The idea of a free pad, free food, unprosecuted dope use, free sex—the world owes them a living—is diametrically opposite to the American dream which created this country. Here are the people who do not want to conform to the norms and mores of our society; many are kids who have lost all respect for themselves, their families, and their country. It is the opinion of the author that this type of ghetto is another social experiment of short duration destined to the same even-

[2] The National Advisory Commission on Civil Disorders, The Kerner Commission, 1969.

tual failure which has ended all Utopian communal schemes in past history.

One must, however, concede that the fallout from this *counter-culture* has been a powerful shaping force in contemporary adolescent psychological orientation.

Perhaps the greatest need of all ghetto areas is a change in the philosophy of life held both by residents there, and by those who live outside the ghetto: this rethinking will be most difficult to change in the direction of greater respect for self and others, of acceptance of internalized responsibility for one's own behavior, obedience to law, hygiene, compassion, charity, and much more involvement by *people who care*. To fail in these directions clearly jeopardizes the total way of life in contemporary America.

An experienced police officer (Texas Department of Public Safety) has contributed the following view of the ghetto, as it is related to a serious facet of criminal activity, namely *Organized Crime in the Ghetto:*

What is a ghetto? How would you describe it to me? One might well answer these questions by saying that it is a blighted area—a community or a neighborhood where people infect one another with the virus of failure, and where young people are infected long before the virus is ever detected or treated to any significant degree.

The crowded, decaying, ramshackled communities in our inner-cities offer little in the way of healthful living conditions for anyone, young or old. They are festering eyesores of a Nation that leads the world in so many areas and they are degrading to every human being who by choice or fate is an inhabitant of them. The ghetto homes, the tenement buildings and shacks, are dirty, deteriorating and unsanitary; yards, where they exist at all, are most often cluttered with broken bottles, junked cars, worn-out refrigerators and trash. Inside the homes and apartments, the residents often lack basic sanitary facilities; hallways are dark, damp, and stacked with garbage. Broken windows go unrepaired and leaking buildings become infested with cockroaches, ants, and rats. Crowded arrangements, due to shifting groups of relatives, friends, or acquaintances, and multiple use of available facilities multiply respiratory infections and communicable diseases. Rickety stairways, improvised stoves, and bad electrical connections take their toll, while infants being bitten by rats are not infrequent happenings.

On the streets of the neighborhood there is little difference from the atmosphere found in the home. Alleys are cluttered with wooden and cardboard crates, old tires, broken bottles, beer cans, wrecked cars, bricks and stenching debris. Condemned buildings, lining the streets, become boarded-up firetraps where addicts shoot, where winos sleep, and where children play. Streets are dirty, the air thick, sooted, and polluted by exhausted emissions, burning trash, the odor of human excretion, and litterings. Parks and recreational facilities are usually inadequate or nonexistent. As a result, the young play in the alleys or on rooftops, or gather in business houses or on street corners because they have no other place to go.

The ghetto, with its steamy, sweaty, and smelly air is a frightening place, especially at night, as it becomes another world—a place not unlike a jungle where Darwin's theory of "survival of the fittest" is a reality and where one only need spend one or two nights to be haunted forever more with the questions: "Are these real people?" "Can we really call this *living*?" Near darkness, the woodwork (tenements) opens up and from it pours sickly human parasites—leeches and suckers of society; those who are involved in full lives of crime—the prostitute, the gambler, the con man, the thief, the addict, and others—those who are always taking from the community and never contributing anything to it in any significant manner. The community once again becomes their number-one victim, and it is an area of the city that can least afford it. Each of those from whom the above steal becomes a loser also, and in turn, so does every member of the community.

The ghetto 'unpeople,' especially the young, inherit the total of those who precede and surround them—their parents, the impoverishment, disappointments, frustrations, fear, and anger. Within them exist a great disparity between the social values to which they aspire and the availability of facilities for acquiring those values in a conventional sort of way.

The ghetto society is not designed to use the limited talents and skills that the young have to offer. Dependence on welfare programs or the obtaining of 'illicit' jobs present the only recognizable opportunity to obtain money by which to satisfy the strong counter-pull in which they find themselves—a conflict situation between what they have learned to need and simultaneously, what they have learned that they should not want or cannot have. The development of crime as an organized way of life is a most marked thing in the ghetto and often times appears to be an 'acceptable' way of life by which the ghetto inhabitant may realize a golden dream.

Psychologists tell us that, as young people, all are drawn to 'hero worship.' We've each experienced our own in the past in middle-class America. But who does the black ghetto member emulate? Who are the every day heroes and idols of the slum child? They are usually, as one might expect, the 'big man' on the streets of their neighborhood. They are the well-fed and the well-dressed:

those who possess big cars, girls, booze, a 'cool pad,' and those who enjoy 'hot connections,' both with other elements of some facet of organized crime and on many occasions, insulation through their association with one or more members of those in positions of authority. These 'heroes' are highly visible in the ghetto in the form of numbers runners, the bookie, the burglar, the fence, the pusher, the loan shark, the prostitute and the pimp . . . all brothers and sisters of the block who, while exhibiting a charismatic style, have risen above their own kind to 'make it' and return to put the big lie on society's claim that 'crime does not pay' in a most eloquent way by flashing big bills and all that it will buy and thereby convincing the young in particular that crime *does* pay, and that it pays very well—particularly if it is properly organized and if the organization has integrity (discipline). Those who are involved in organized aspects of crime in the ghetto are looked upon as models of success and shining examples for others to follow for they have acquired 'status.' Don't all Americans admire success and status? Certainly they do! Is there any reason then to believe that the ghetto young are any different or any less American than we are? I think not.

If there is any surprise at all in the story of the ghetto it must surely be that only about ten percent of its young become involved in lives of crime and not ninety to one hundred percent of them. This one statistic alone should be an indicator that there is still much hope for those unfortunate persons who were born not only as members of a minority group but also into a depressed area of our Nation if—*if* sincere efforts are made to correct present inadequacies and to open new channels or wide existing ones to allow the ghetto resident, especially the young, to be a part of, to participate in 'the system,' and to be a qualified recipient of their fair share of society's rewards.

Another primary source contribution is offered for its valid and timely insights into racism in the ghetto, which is perhaps of the greatest importance to understanding the ghetto:

As Personnel Director of the —— Police Department I learned first hand of many of the misconceptions held by members of the minority groups. In an effort to recruit Blacks for the department, I held on-campus rap sessions with groups of senior students at a local Black college. The students all expressed a fear of police officers that appeared inherent. A large number actually believed that a Black police officer could not arrest a white person—that the Black officer was used solely for policing Blacks; consequently, they had no respect for Black officers and had no desire to become officers themselves. The group viewed the police as occupation troops in their neighborhoods, whose sole purpose was to harass them and restrict their liberties. When I reminded them that the crime rate in largely minority neighborhoods was extremely disproportionately high—that the people who could less afford the loss of personal property were the ones who suffered the greater loss and that more of their neighbors were assaulted, raped and robbed than in all the remaining part of the city, they appeared to be astounded. They seemed to see the role of the police in a new light after considering how bad it could be without the police. They were later polled as to whether they desired more or fewer policemen assigned to their neighborhood and a large majority expressed a desire for more officers.

The same groups complained that white officers did not seem to understand the problems of the Blacks. They were told that this was precisely why we were attempting to hire more Blacks—so that we would have more officers who did understand their problems and could work to solve them more effectively. They were told that nowhere in society could they contribute more, as individuals, to improve society than as officers, on the streets, where the problems are.

After dialogue with them, an interest was kindled which is paying dividends in recruitment efforts and in mutual understanding between the police and the minority public.

The —— Police Department has increased its efforts to create more understanding between minority members and the police by creating Community Service Centers staffed by policemen and assisted by para-police who are members of the community. Many people in lower income areas have more problems than in affluent areas. These may be Police related problems or they may be problems concerning city, county or state. One of the main responsibilities of the Community Service Officer is to aid these people in finding the right place to resolve these problems. A case in point concerned a fourteen year old boy with a severe eye problem. His family did not have enough money to buy glasses so the boy just didn't go to school. The Community Service Officer talks and visits with other people such as school principals, social workers, pastors, etc. He gets tips on people with problems and goes to them and *offers help*. This offer creates a good taste for the police. The officer visited the family of the boy with the vision problem to see if he could help. The officer found that the family was deserving and was trying very hard to subsist without going on welfare. The officer found out that the Lions Club has a fund with which to buy glasses and to pay for examinations for needy children. After the examination, it was found that the boy was considered legally blind by State standards. A call was made to the State Commission for the Blind and the boy was assigned to a caseworker who followed up on all the boy's needs.

Many people are too proud to ask for help. By talking to people in the neighborhood, school teachers, truant officers, and other police officers, the Community Services Officer can find many areas where he can be of assistance without being asked. To sum it up, the Community Service Officer becomes a 'part' of the area he is in and tries to be of assistance to the people who live in 'his' district. He attempts to 'Do unto others as he would have them do unto him.'

This type program helps to minimize or erase their bad conception of the police based on hearsay or past experiences where the police are contacted only in an enforcement capacity, and where, many times, officer's actions reinforce the concept that the police are their enemy.

While most police administrators agree that the Community Service Center concept is beneficial toward improving police-citizen relations, they are increasingly aware that the attitudes of policemen must change. Charges of police brutality have become increasingly widespread and now not only include complaints of physical abuse but also the use of insulting, threatening, derogatory, demeaning, or racist language. To combat this, the —— Police Department has issued a written order, which is strictly enforced, which prohibits the use of the terms 'boy' or 'girl' when addressing adults. The order also prohibits the substitution of words like 'Kike' for Jew, 'Spick' for Mexican-American, or 'Nigger' for Negro. Of course, officers are severely disciplined or terminated for the use of unnecessary physical force.

It has been my experience that whatever bias an officer possesses when he joins a force, without adequate training, often gets worse. Officers see the worst side of life, and in view of the higher crime rate in the ghetto, their stereotypes of minority members are greatly strengthened. Such prejudices are usually fortified by close association with other officers who have had the same experience.

A final view, contributed in late 1972 by a police officer, is the result of his personal experience in the Ghetto. It is quoted, not for its unusual insights, but for its truthful observations which many officers have experienced.

I am a police officer for the city of ———. During my first two and one-half years of service I worked as a patrol officer and a field training officer in a section of the city known as the Ghetto. I had never before been exposed to this type of neighborhood or associated with minority people. This experience did not make me an expert on the subject but I did gain much knowledge on it. I had many dealings with the youthful offender during this time. Most families in this area are very large. The parents do not appear to care about controlling childbirth. A large percentage of the people live as common-law husband and wife. When they get tired of each other they separate and move in with someone else and when the children grow up they usually don't even know who their father is. In many families both mother and father work. Since there is no one to take care of the younger children, many times an older child is left at home to babysit instead of going to school.

There are more cases of truancy in this type of neighborhood than in other parts of the city. Truants are a great problem to the police because the largest amount of daytime burglaries are done by youths roaming the streets during school hours. It is very hard to recruit minority group officers because of the lack of education or the lack of interest in the profession. Many black officers are looked down on because their people think of them as traitors.

It is difficult to say what can be done to improve the problems of the Ghetto. Many things have been tried and many things are being tried. We can only hope that someday there will not be such a thing as a Ghetto or racism.

Social malise caused by the ghettos of the world are of sufficient gravity to pose a threat to the continued existence of modern society. *Mickey-Mouse, band-aid* solutions (billions have been spent in recent years), have been shown to be unable to abort the pernicious fallout of the social asphyxia, dyscontrol, and deterioration resulting from the ghetto. Nothing short of an all-out mobilization, as for war, is believed to have any chance against the long course of social neglect and exploitation which has produced the ghetto. Time is running out rapidly. It is to be hoped that individual citizens, business, industry, labor, and government will promptly allocate the interest and means necessary to cope with this cancer of our society, the *dark ghetto*.

CHAPTER XIII

CONCLUSION

POLICE CORRECTIONAL workers, and social workers interact every day, every hour, with the entire spectrum of humanity and are practicing psychologists, whether they realize it or not.

Both criminal and non-criminal (civil) type behaviors are by social directive the responsibility of these agencies. Professionals in human relations cannot function without the essential insights modern science has discovered relative to the nature and motivations of human behavior. No longer may *odd* behavior be glibly explained away by yesterday's myths relative to inherited moral depravity or predestined determinism, from environmental distortions of reality, or social accidents. Instead, a dispassionate consideration of the developmental causes of deviate behavior and criminal manifestations of it, from both psychological and sociological aspects, is essential. Half of all deviate behavior is found in the age bracket of six to under twenty-one.

The next step is to be able to recognize the presence of psychological factors in an officer-citizen encounter—an adversary confrontation or a social assistance act. Finally, the appropriate action which is professionally indicated will, hopefully, be considered. Obviously, no *cookbook recipe* is useable in interpersonal operations involving deviant behavior; it is hoped, however, that essential insights can be gained from a book such as this in order to minimize malpractices; to reduce harm to maladjusted persons; to salvage as much as possible from dangerous and damaged cases; and to improve the mental hygiene of the individual officer or parent as a person, as a family man, and as a public servant.

The human brain is in many respects like a data processing machine: it receives, classifies, stores, and retrieves information (input) from sensory receptors; this memory bank (stream of consciousness) is what we use to cope with life's adjustment requirements and as feedback correction for new learnings and behavior.

The human brain, an organ of the body, is subject to the same physical laws as other organs. Organic conditions which are positively related to mental illness are: genetic defects or birth injury; brain tumor; arteriosclerosis (hardening of the arteries with poor oxygen supply to the brain tissues) and degenerative diseases of senility; diseases of the brain (syphilis); trauma to the brain (blows, falls, concussions); toxic substances (chronic alcoholism, drug damage, lead or gas); nutritional deficiencies and endocrine troubles; after-effects of many diseases affecting brain tissue; and organic damage to brain area related to emotional stress.

Another category of mental illness, called functional because the sick person is unable to function efficiently, has no identifiable physical evidence of organic defect. However, the victim can be as sick as with an organic condition, although such organic defect may not be demonstrable—even in autopsy. Some combination of organic and functional causal factors is usually found in severe mental illness.

Mental illness today is recognized as a legitimate form of illness and the stigma from this category of illness is not what it used to be. However, for many people the mysterious nature of mental illness and its understanding and acceptance by the general public is still far from universal. Great need exists for the general public to realize that most mental illness is mild, temporary in nature, almost all cases are treatable, and that full recovery is to be expected in almost all cases—except some five percent which are severe, chronic, or psychotic in nature.

The simple facts are that each of us is not *normal* all the time, that we all have mental hygiene conditions ranging from some shade of gray, from very dark and sick to very light and relatively adjusted emotional states. Every person can be brought to a condition of breakdown (emotional collapse) if the stress is severe enough and applied long enough; there is no superhuman person who can cope forever with intolerable stress. War experience has shown that psychiatric casualties are unavoidable if prolonged severe stress is allowed to persist.

Unconscious psychodynamic motivations as well as the possibility of mental illness must be considered in the study of the juvenile offender. Compulsive theft is an example of unconscious psychodynamic motivations based on hostility and aggression, perhaps elements related to seeking of self-punishment (masochism); desire for sexual thrill; seeking to hurt parents, spouse and/or family; ventilating of hostility; and surfacing of compulsions to hurt, destroy, and vandalize.

The influence of heredity in explanations of organic relationship to behavior cannot be ignored. Studies of the incidence of psychotic conditions among identical twins show that some personality disturbances are definitely related to inherited physical defects; and inferior equipment to meet the stress of living is, regrettably, what some individuals receive from their ancestors.

Individual resistance to stress obviously depends upon a combination of hereditary and enviornmental factors as shaped by social conditioning. One must note that environmental shaping is of the greatest importance in the etiology of criminal behavior; we are not born to be criminals, drunkards, or addicts. We are born into an environment with differential exposure to crime or non-crime factors as shapers of behavior.

Both heredity and environment operate with each of us. Defects related to birth, accidents, injuries, aging, and diseases affecting neural tissue, as well as the absorption of toxic substances, are clearly of organic nature. Thus, we have many sources of causal factors in deviant behavior: heredity, environment, organic disease resulting in mental illness. Each of these areas has been explored by experts in every field. And yet we still have the problem of the juvenile offender—no one has yet come up with a fool-proof solution for the eradication of this blight on society. Perhaps the key may be found in a summation by Dr. Sherman R. Day of Georgia State University:[1]

> We are different from most criminal offenders in one way. Somewhere in our upbringing, someone taught us, and we were able to grasp the concept, that for every action there is a reaction. We learned that when we choose an alternative, there is a consequence to that alternative. And further, that if we do not like the consequence of that choice, the key to changing the consequence is the person himself. That is, the person, and *only* the person, has the capacity to direct his own destiny.

Society can provide the tools for learning, the sanctions for abuse of the law, motivation for abiding by the law, facilities for rehabilitation after the offense—but in the final analysis, it is the juvenile offender himself who must resolve the age-old question of self-choice, and has the most power to overcome difficulties, handicaps, or deprivations, in the face of all handicaps; it is he alone who is in control of his destiny.

This condensed over-view of two of the most accepted theories to explain human behavior (Freudian and Skinnerian) is not intended to be an adequate canvass; as research pushes back the ignorance of man as he understands himself today, undoubtedly other more comprehensive formulations will be advanced. The tragedy of man as he engages in war, crime, family dissolution, violence, neglect of hygiene, and superstition must somehow be aborted: each generation must not be condemned to repeat the mistakes of the previous one, like two mirrors locked face to face down an endless corridor of despair. Let us hope man can learn to respect his fellowman and live as *men of goodwill.*

A serious question confronts American society today: can the protection of the public be performed adequately by the criminal justice system as it now operates? The Latin phrase: *Salus populi suprema lex* (The welfare of the people is the supreme law) no longer obtains, particularly in urban areas. More precisely, the breakdown of law observance and enforcement most evidenced by the youthful offender (ages 15–25) in militancy, drug abuse, vicious racism, and violent

[1] Sixth Annual Interagency Workshop of Contemporary Corrections and the Behavioral Sciences, Sam Houston State University, Huntsville, Texas, June 1971.

irrational criminal acts, is the number one social problem today in America and in many other countries. No ostrich-like blindness can hide the seriousness of this threat to civilization; the problem is real, it is immediate, and it demands solution. Failing in this, the continued existence of today's social order is in grave jeopardy.

APPENDIX

The following six questions were answered by students in my class during the fall semester, 1972. They show insights which were sought as objectives by the author and as perceived by the present generation with today's orientation.

1. THE JUVENILE OFFENDER: *WHO* IS HE?

The juvenile offender is anyone who commits a crime or anti-social act that is still legally a juvenile. Generally this includes people below 18 years of age. Recently we've seen the young at age of 7 years involved with drugs and theft. The age span of the juvenile offender seems to get broader. In America, half of the crimes reported in the 1970's are committed by people under the age of 18.

* * *

He is a person, usually between the ages of seven and whatever is considered to be the age of adults—in the State in which one resides—who has either been adjudicated delinquent or found guilty of violations of the law. Perhaps he is merely responsible for behavior which is considered detrimental to the best interests of himself or other members of either his own or the adult society in which he lives. Most of these people are males; however, females are more frequently becoming guilty of types of behavior which may be considered irresponsible.

He moves within a subculture which may have created a milieu of morality in which violations of the establishment norms of behavior have positive connotations—and in which he is encouraged by feedback which reinforces acting-out behavior which is contrary to the long range best interests of himself and the groups of ideas against which he is reacting. He is a person nearly physically mature who is trying to focus his energies in a manner which actually bears greater resemblance to a child than an adult.

121

He is usually a male offender, and engages in an increasing amount of crime each year. He is sometimes, but not as a rule, in a position of wealth or power. He is a young person between the ages of 10 and 18 or 21 who has not been acculturated. He has not learned the basic values of society in an internal sense, and he rebels at the *straight* world. He, most often than not, commits crimes in the company of others like himself. He is of average intelligence and body type, although the Gluecks found a slight predominance of athletic types in their delinquency studies. He is also likely to be a school drop-out. If he is black or Mexican-American, he suffers a greater risk of becoming delinquent than if he is white.

* * *

Boys aged 10–17, girls aged 12–16, one-half are 6–21 who commit index offenses. He may be in counterculture groups such as drug addicts.

A young teen who has been brought up and feels no conscious wrong in what he does. He really doesn't know who he is. His id—pleasure principle most of the time—takes over his ego—reality and most of the time super-ego—(that concerned with conscious and social factors) doesn't influence his behavior.

* * *

The juvenile offender is technically defined as a male between the ages of 12 and 18, or a female between the ages of 12 and 17, that violates a law, federal or state. But he is more than that. He is a person who may or may not have been caught. I think that probably every person who has ever lived, could at some time during his delinquent years be classified as a juvenile offender, for we have all broken a law, social or written, at some time during these years. Here we are concerned with the less fortunate ones. The ones that have been caught, that society is aware of.

The offender usually comes from a broken home, cares for no one but himself, will not go to school, may be violent at times, show signs of hostility, egocentric gratification, or he may be arrogant or rebellious.

* * *

2. THE JUVENILE OFFENDER: *WHAT* IS HE?

The juvenile offender is an anti-social, alienated youth. He rejects the present social norms and adopts attitudes of indifference and aggression. He isn't concerned with the result of his actions and he will be aggressive when necessary to get what he wants. He lives on the spur of the moment impulse. His desires are his motivation for his actions. Reason isn't used. Morals and ethics are something he expects to be treated with but he doesn't give a thought to a morally wrong action.

He is generally a product of his environment. His parental guidance was so lacking that he has adopted a hedonistic attitude. His life is self-centered. Long range goals are lacking. His life is so meaningless that this furthers his frustration and he more ardently pursues his hedonistic style.

* * *

He is a source of irritation to law enforcement and to the general society. He is a waste to society in many ways: he does not get a complete education, probably will not hold a responsible job, does not enter the Armed Forces, does not accept the main values of society, and does not seek help for his predicament. He drains money from the economy in the form of all the services rendered for him or to him in the juvenile justice system. He has sometimes become a threat to life and property in public schools, large cities, and occasionally small towns. He has increasingly become a drug user, which may boost his crime potential if he takes expensive drugs. Last but not least, he is likely to become an adult offender if he continues in his accustomed life pattern.

* * *

The offender may be, and probably is, sick. This may be either psychological or physical or both. This person may be psychotic, rebellious, refusing to adjust to the society, but rather, wanting society to adjust to him.

The juvenile is a problem of society and must be coped with. He can be helped through re-education, rehabilitation and reintegration.

The one thing we must not forget is that juvenile offenders are human beings and with the correct medication they can be returned to useful and productive individuals, and eventually adults. The offender may be an un-person—uneducated, unclean, unhealthy, unemployed, and unwilling to change. He may not care about anything or anybody but himself. But he can be helped.

* * *

He is the child of a society which is also in a great state of flux— more likely than not the natural product of a set of environmental circumstances which contain greater than normal odds of producing an individual whose natural reactions to his environment will be to destroy the situation he grew up in. He is the cause of much crime which occupies the activities of his local police department —the reason for the existence of the entire concept of the juvenile court system—perhaps the bane of his parent's existence—though this is not necessarily so. Some parents would prefer not to learn even his whereabouts. . . .

He is a young person whose greatest threat to life is the danger of his own suicide. He may become a resident in the juvenile detention system . . . where he is less likely than elsewhere to gain control of his life. . . . He is the victim of his own powerful emotional drive to find a place for himself, contentment, a way of life, a style of life, a satisfactory sexual adjustment. Lacking the maturity and opportunities an older person might have to cope with the same problems—he becomes the problem.

* * *

3. THE JUVENILE OFFENDER: *WHERE* IS HE?

He is usually located in a broken home. He normally flourishes in large cities where control over his behavior is more difficult. He is more often found in inner-city and ghetto areas. If apprehended, he can be found in juvenile court, in detention homes, in half-way houses, in reform schools and other facilities provided for him by the state. In general, he is in a big mess. He has lately found his way into the spotlight of public attention.

* * *

He may be a resident of the state department of corrections, the juvenile detention system, the state hospital, the unfortunate occupant of the county jail in the absence of more appropriate detention facilities—and every small town and large city which contains people of his age group. He may be found trespassing on government property or smoking marijuana in his own bedroom; shoplifting with his friends or planning with a warped mind a lonely suicide or murder. . . . He is frequently found in a car—likely as not, somebody elses. He may be next door or 3,000 miles from him in a commune which he hopes will conceal his whereabouts from his parents. He may be in school, or he may not have been for years—though the odds that he will find destructive behavior appealing decreases with the time spent in school. . . . Should he ever become a resident of the State Department of Corrections he will find most of his companions have not graduated from high school.

He may be found throughout history. The early Greeks and Romans were also concerned about the behavior of their young people.

He is anywhere along the social ladder. From the poverty-ridden ghetto, or middle class, and even the upper class of society. Mentally, he is where he thinks he can belong. Physically, he's on the street, hanging around pool halls, street corners—anywhere, he can be at the moment. Finally he is in a patrol car, then to juvenile court, and into a reformatory. If the process has reached this far, he may be nowhere. He is always where he isn't wanted. The place where he should have been since he was born—in a good home where he can be provided for, cared for, guided correctly, and most important loved—is absent.

The juvenile offender in the final analysis is the real unperson—unwanted, unloved, under developed in many areas of his own maturation process.

* * *

He is found where almost 80 percent of crime is, in the Ghettos. He meets all the *street* people there. Most often he is in metropolitan areas where there is over crowding, insufficient recreation and unhealthy places.

Most of the time you find a juvenile whose been *caught* in detention homes, trade schools, or behind bars.

Where there is a sick parent, you find a sick child.

* * *

4. THE JUVENILE OFFENDER: *WHEN* IS HE?

In the last two decades the rate of delinquency has greatly risen. You have delinquents when there is overcrowding. When there isn't prepared convenient recreation, when people, or his family don't give him the 3 L's: love, limitations, and let them grow up. You have a delinquent when he's been battered because of anal elimination, or a father transfers his own problems to the child, severe punishment.

* * *

He exists whenever society has not prepared itself to cope with the erratic emotional states of young people—whenever there is a vacuum in the life space that must be immediately filled in the mind of the person who feels a lack. He exists when parents are too busy, or too over protective; when young people must be alone—or when they are together. He is the accomplishment of conscious rearing and total negligence—because the factors which go into influencing the behavior of a society are difficult to interpret and more difficult to understand. He becomes dangerous to society when opportunity for destructive behavior coincides with subtle psychological drives and motivations common to all young people—and when proper responses to emotional demands have not been conditioned adequately enough to enable him to find instead a proper outlet for his behavior.

* * *

5. THE JUVENILE OFFENDER: *WHY* IS HE?

He is shaped into delinquency when his life is full of negative factors. A ghetto, poor diet, no stimulation, poor examples, no guidance, no help or love, a poor education, no place to spend his idle time, poor companionship, no parents with anything to offer; then we have a juvenile offender who is trained to be that way.

* * *

He may exist simply because his parents have not been able to discover an adequate way of meeting their own needs. . . . The unwilling victim of smother love—or rejected, when he should have been accepted—undisciplined by a father figure; left too much to his own devices by one or both parents; discouraged by what he sees society as consisting of, he seeks to preserve himself by destroying what he thinks has caused the situation. He may be the unconscious victim of his own drives—never realizing he will destroy himself long before he will ever change anything else.

* * *

6. WHAT HAVE BEEN THE OBJECTIVES (AIMS) OF THIS COURSE?

The aims of this course have been to acquaint the student with the environmental and psychological causes of destructive behavior in young people. . . . We have probed the larger society of the unpeople of the ghetto, the smaller society of the family, the educational community, and the peer group with a view toward discovering the long-range effects of these institutions as well as discovering ways some of these influences might be altered for the better.

We have discussed the psychological discoveries of Freud, the implications of our unconscious motivation, the efficacy of the Skinnerian approach to behavioral conditioning and have been reminded of the physiological problems connected with behavior—brain damage from disease, senility, and the long range influence of maternal nutritional deprivation.

This course was designed to help us see the child as an omnibus in which all of his life experience and ancestry ride.

* * *

We need to re-establish America's personal goals. We need an emphasis on respect, consideration, love and emotion. At present we are inner-directed toward monetary values. If we continue in a hedonistic direction we will continue in the juvenile delinquent-crime world we have established.

INSTRUCTOR'S MANUAL

Introduction
Objectives
Methods
Audio-Visual Teaching Aids
Quiz and Examination Materials
Sample Quiz
Sample Final Exam

INTRODUCTION

An instructor's manual for any textbook should justify its printing and careful consideration by using instructors. The author's experience with the subject matter and familiarity with teaching aids related to the text should qualify him for such a task.

This manual parallels the format of the text in that it avoids wordiness and covers only basic essentials. In no sense is it to be considered as a prescription to be followed without modification by the instructor. It is suggestive, only, based on the author's recent decade of teaching precisely this subject matter to thousands of college-level pre- and in-service students in police, corrections and social rehabilitation courses related to behavioral science.

The author's four decades of experience as a professional educator is condensed herein; hopefully its contents will merit consideration for planning and classroom application. Ideas and insights have been classroom-tested, revised, and found to be practicable and effective with both experienced (in-service) and beginning students of behavioral science.

Each instructor is encouraged to develop and perfect his own teaching methodology. One true axiom for effective teaching is that the more the student does for himself the more he will learn. A maximum of classroom participation and of discussion is to be encouraged. The usual lecture is the poorest teaching method ever devised. When electricity came into the classroom a revolution in educational methods became possible. A heavy use of multi-sensory aids to learning is recommended. Particularly where classes meet once a week for a three-hour session, showing one of the suggested films will be found to have great merit; each recommended film has been selected with recency and excellence of content as criteria.

The quiz and examination questions are also furnished solely as suggestions; up-dating, rearrangement, and adaptation to local conditions is recommended. The nature of this social science subject matter is that it is constantly changing in today's fluid society; instructors are urged to use locally available examples and contemporary cases. A newspaper of national circulation will be an essential reference, for example, *The Christian Science Monitor, The National Observer,* or *The New York Times.*

No list of reference books is given for the reason that the subject matter of this course is highly fluid and must be constantly up dated. Most books which are two years in print are already antedated. The National Clearinghouse for Mental Health Information of the U.S. Department of Health, Education and Welfare has produced two excellent publications: *Abstracts of the Complete Psychological Works of Sigmund Freud* and *Youth in Turmoil;* both are recommended for basic parallel reading by both instructors and students.

OBJECTIVES

The text's unique subject matter selection and style of presentation required that only *essential* behavioral insights be included. It is written for easy assimilation by typical college and police academy students, and a concise yet adequate canvass of the chapter headings has been attempted.

The text is believed to have especial merit for sensitizing new entrants in social service fields to the peculiar social forces operating in the inner-city.

The text covers the essential social psychological insights believed necessary for initial safety-minimum role enactment by beginners in social service work as they interface with youth whether in adversary or helping encounters. In-service officers will profit from its insights to the nature, motivations and criminogenic factors operating in today's youths.

The objective of the text is to provide a readable, terse, yet scientifically sound presentation of the who, what, when, and how of the behavior of today's youthful offender.

METHODS

Perhaps the most criticized aspect of professional education is its emphasis on methodology. The author believes method of instruction is important; learning efficiency can be improved by psychologically sound teaching methods.

The first essential is for the student to be active and individually committed to the learning task at hand. All learning is self-learning. The best instructor can only contrive learning experiences which the learner must work with and react to. Specifically for this course, the essential requirement is for the student to read as widely and intensively as possible the excellent books, periodicals, and newspapers easily available today in college and public libraries and which provide an embarrassment of riches for parallel reading.

Students will find that writing critical evaluations, and additions to chapters, based both on their parallel readings and on their personal experiences will be a challenging and rewarding exercise. The text has been written, in part, by exactly this procedure.

The films listed have been selected for individual excellence. New films are constantly being produced; the task of remaining *au courant* with film output will require the instructor to keep his name on mailing lists from producers and distributors (university film libraries and state film repositories), and from the U.S. Government's National Audio-Visual Center, National Archives and Records Service, Washington, D.C. 20409. Extensive use of films is recommended. We are living in an age when most students have been conditioned to learn easily from films, and many recent and excellent films are becoming available in social psychology.

A final word relative to methodology: the author believes that effective classroom learning largely depends on the fullest participation and expression of ideas by students; "talking at" students is poor pedagogy. The more the students are active, the more they will learn and retain. The text should not be the sole source of ideas; it is designed as a point of departure for amplification—its brevity compels such use.

AUDIO VISUAL TEACHING AIDS

Angry Boy, Mental Health Film Board Series, International Film Bureau Co.

Aquamarine to Diamonds, Las Palmas School for Girls, Henry F. Greenberg Productions, Los Angeles, California. Available from Hollywood Film Company, 956 Seward St., Hollywood, Calif. 90038.

(1) *Children Without* (2) *The Time of Their Lives,* National Education Association Division of Press, Radio and Television, 1201 16th Street, North West, Washington, D.C. 20036.

The Dangerous Years, Kemper Insurance, Modern Talking Picture Service Incorporated, 4084 Westhemer Road, Houston, Texas 77027.

Every Hour, Every Day, International Association of Chiefs of Police, 11 First Field Road, Gaithersburg, Md. 20760.

Gateways to the Mind, Bell Telephone Company.

Help, I'm a Cop, Instructional Dynamics Inc., 166 East Superior Street, Chicago, Illinois 60611.

Journey In Time, NBC Documentary, 1970, (drug culture, glue, heroin)

Law and Order, Zipporah Films, 54 Lewis Wharf, Boston, Massachusetts 02110.

Mind of Man, Indiana University Audio-Visual Center, Bloomington, Indiana 47401.

Miracle of the Mind, McGraw-Hill Films, Manchester Road, Manchester, Missouri 63011.

No Gun Towers, No Fences, Indiana University, Audio-Visual Center, Bloomington, Indiana 47401.

Not All Cops, Not All Kids, Design Center, 1611 Connecticut Avenue, North West, Washington, D.C. 20009.

No Jail Can Change Me, University of California, Extension Media Center, Berkeley, California 84720.

The Odds Against, America Foundation Institute of Corrections, 1532 Philadelphia National Bank Building, Philadelphia, Pennsylvania 19107.

The Price of a Life, America Foundation Institute of Corrections, 1532 Philadelphia National Bank Building, Philadelphia, Pennsylvania 19107.

The Revolving Door, America Foundation Institute of Corrections, 1532 Philadelphia National Bank Building, Philadelphia, Pennsylvania 19107.

B.F. Skinner Films: "Business, Behaviorism and the Bottom Line", *A Conversation with B.F. Skinner,* and *Token Economy: Behaviorism Applied, Psychology Today Films,* CRM Educational Films, Del Mar, California 92014.

"Psychology Today Films": (1) *Personality* (2) *Abnormal Behavior,* CRM Productions, 9263 Third Street, Beverly Hills, California 90210 (Rental).

Shades of Gray, U.S. Army Medical Department Film No. 5047 (now officially obsolete, but much still of great value) Purchase available at $114.75 from U.S. Army.

SAMPLE QUIZ

DEFINE BRIEFLY THE FOLLOWING TERMS:

1. "Smother Love"—

2. Alienation—

3. Generation Gap—

4. The key ideas of Dr. Freud (List 5)—

5. Glueck's delinquency predictor factors (List 5)—

6. Existentialism —

7. Physiological Age—

8. Role Theory—

9. Acting Out Behavior (with example)—

10. Functional mental illness—

11. Cybernetics—

12. Psyche and soma—(define each and tell how related)—

13. Psychosomatic illness—

14. Unconscious psychodynamic motivation (with example)—

15. Organicity—

16. Stress—

17. Mental Age (M.A.)—

18. Psychopathology—

19. "Programmed" life style—

20. Pathogenic or criminogenic family setting—

21. Personality—

22. List 10 typical characteristics of adolescents—
    1.   6.
    2.   7.
    3.   8.
    4.   9.
    5.   10.

23. What are the "Three L's?"

24. What is "Condition Red?"

25. Explain the "Oedipus Complex"—

SAMPLE FINAL EXAM

FORM B

DIRECTIONS: Answer briefly, *adequately*, in space provided.

1. List twenty (20) typical characteristics of today's adolescent:

2. Why have some juvenile courts failed to achieve their hoped-for goals?

3. Discuss psychological explanations relative to sexual deviancy.

4. What are the apparent comsequences for both adolescents and society from drug and alcohol abuse?

5. What is today's humanistic attitude toward traditional "punishment" as correction for juvenile criminal acts?

6. How may the serious anti-social effects of negative peer group power be minimized?

7. How may the ghetto's criminogenic environment be aborted?

8. The "school" as a social institution is in trouble. Explain.

9. What are the central ideas of Freudian theory as related to adolescents?

10. How must today's family as a social institution be improved?

INDEX

143